I0089349

DEBRA OSWALD is a writer for stage, film, television and children's fiction.

Her stage plays have been produced around Australia. *Gary's House*, *Sweet Road* and *The Peach Season* were all shortlisted for the NSW Premier's Award, and her play *Dags* has had many Australian productions. *Gary's House* has been performed in translation in Denmark and Japan.

Mr Bailey's Minder broke the Griffin Theatre's box office record in 2004, toured nationally in 2006, and was produced in Philadelphia in 2008.

Debra has written three plays for Australian Theatre for Young People (ATYP)—*Skate*, *Stories in the Dark* (NSW Premier's Literary Play Award in 2008) and *House on Fire* (2010). Eight of Debra's plays are published by Currency Press.

She is the co-creator and head writer of the award-winning Channel Ten series *Offspring*. Debra won the 2011 NSW Premier's Literary Award for the *Offspring* telemovie script and won the 2014 AACTA for Best Television Screenplay for an episode in series 4. Her other television credits include award-winning episodes of *Police Rescue*, *Palace of Dreams*, *The Secret Life of Us*, *Sweet and Sour* and *Bananas in Pyjamas*.

She is the author of three 'Aussie Bite' books for kids, including *Nathan and the Ice Rockets*, and six novels for teenage readers including *The Redback Leftovers* and *Blue Noise*.

Her first novel for adults, *Useful*, will be published by Penguin in 2015.

Beejan Olfat (left background) as Mitchell, Mike Hamer as Travis and Jarryd Kirwan (foreground) as JT in the 2003 atyp production. (Photo: Phil Sheather)

skate

debra
oswald

Currency Press, Sydney

CURRENCY PLAYS

Skate first published in 2004
by Currency Press Pty Ltd,
PO Box 2287, Strawberry Hills, NSW, 2012, Australia
enquiries@currency.com.au
www.currency.com.au

Reprinted 2009, 2011, 2015.

Copyright © Debra Oswald, 2003.

Copying for Educational Purposes

The Australian *Copyright Act 1968* (Act) allows a maximum of one chapter or 10% of this book, whichever is the greater, to be copied by any educational institution for its educational purposes provided that that educational institution (or the body that administers it) has given a remuneration notice to Copyright Agency Limited (CAL) under the Act.

For details of the CAL licence for educational institutions contact CAL, 15/233 Castlereagh Street, Sydney, NSW, 2000. Tel: (02) 9394 7600; Fax: (02) 9394 7601; E-mail: info@copyright.com.au.

Copying for Other Purposes

Except as permitted under the Act, for example a fair dealing for the purposes of study, research, criticism or review, no part of this book may be reproduced, stored in a retrieval system, or transmitted in any form or by any means without prior written permission. All inquiries should be made to the publisher at the address above.

Any performance or public reading of *Skate* is forbidden unless a licence has been received from the author or the author's agent. The purchase of this book in no way gives the purchaser the right to perform the play in public, whether by means of a staged production or a reading. All applications for public performance should be addressed to the playwright c/- Cameron's Management, Locked Bag 848, Surry Hills NSW 2010; tel: 02 9319 7199; email: info@cameronsmanagement.com.au.

In accordance with the requirement of the Australian Media, Entertainment & Arts Alliance, Currency Press has made every effort to identify, and gain permission of, the artists who appear in the photographs which illustrate these plays.

Cataloguing-in-publication data for this title is available from the National Library of Australia website: www.nla.gov.au

Publication of this title was assisted by the Commonwealth Government through the Australia Council, its arts funding and advisory body.

Set by Dean Nottle.
Cover design by Kate Florance, Currency Press.
Front cover shows Blake Bowden as Corey in the 2003 ATYP production. (Photo: Phil Sheather)

CONTENTS

Currency Press acknowledges the Traditional Owners of the Country on which we live and work. We pay our respects to all Aboriginal and Torres Strait Islander Elders, past and present.

For the kids of Deniliquin and the people who care about them.

PLAYWRIGHT'S NOTE

DEBRA OSWALD

Sometimes writers get lucky. I got lucky in 2002 when the Australian Theatre for Young People (atyp) offered me the chance to write this play.

atyp were intrigued by events that happened in a town in south-western New South Wales—a group of kids battled for years to get a skatepark built and, in the middle of that, were hit with the sudden death of one of their friends. I took on the job of writing a fictional play inspired by that story. It's a story which is echoed in many communities—in towns where kids have fought for skateparks and towns where kids have been hit by the death of a teenager, from suicide, road accidents and so on.

atyp sent me and the director, Timothy Jones, to Deniliquin for two weeks to do research. I love research—especially live, stickybeak research where you talk to people, not just relying on books or the net. If there's any excuse to get out of my house and do research for a play, I'll grab the chance. For various scripts over the years, I've hitched a lift on a Police Rescue Squad truck, driven out west to trudge around on a salt lake, loitered on a peach farm, sat in synagogue for a bar mitzvah, interrogated strangers in pubs and so on.

For two weeks, I set up house in my little onsite caravan on the banks of the Edwardes River in Deni. Tim and I spent most of every day hanging around the skatepark, yacking to skaters, BMXers and their friends. Or we parked ourselves in a café in Deni and interviewed the school principal, parents, youth worker, town mayor, police, teachers and others. We found that people were amazingly generous with their time and their stories.

Towards the end of our stay, Tim and I spent a couple of afternoons holed up in an old theatre in Deni, a building which reeked of possum piss. There, we thrashed out story possibilities and ways to tell the story, with me raving and marching around the hall. Intoxicated by the possum fumes, we convinced ourselves we had a pretty good story—a story about friendship, about prejudice and the power of perseverance. And about the moment when it really hits you in the guts that life isn't always fair.

Skate is also a story embedded in the culture of teenage boys—a culture which is often marginalised instead of celebrated for its strengths. I get very sick of the way boys are so often put down and shamed. (Many people would prefer to shove all boys in a bunker when they hit 12 and not let them out until they turn 20 or so.)

Skateboarding is a good example of those attitudes. So many people are prejudiced against skaters—all they see are 'drug-dealing gangs', chaos, danger and droopy shorts—a long way from the truth. I'm not saying that skaters are all angels and there are never any problems. But the reality you would see at most skateparks is pretty positive: groups of guys—some girls but mostly guys—hanging around together, doing a thing they love, with amazing harmony. Skating and BMXing may be unstructured but there are unspoken rules and goodwill operating, so skateparks usually have a kind of happy anarchy. Big guys teaching little kids to do tricks, the discipline to work at a trick to get it right, skaters taking turns on runs, genuine appreciation for the talent of another skater, plus that fantastic teasing and self-mocking humour of Australian teenage boys.

I came home and wrote a draft of the play—*Skate*—and worked on redrafts with Tim and atyp Artistic Director David Berthold. Then early in 2003, Tim auditioned nearly 80 atyp performers to find 14 actors to play roles aged from 12 to 40, half of whom had to be able to skateboard or at least fake it okay. I think we found a wonderful cast in the end.

We also ended up with a brilliant set which turned into a half-pipe skateramp by the last scene. How excellent to have skateboarding on stage—much more fun that characters sitting around on couches chatting for an entire play.

After the Sydney season of *Skate*, atyp organised a country tour—to take the show back to the district that inspired it. The cast and crew did seven one-night stands—in Hillston, Hay, Balranald, Barham, Deniliquin, Echuca and Finley.

It was a difficult exercise—bumping a big set (with skateramps) into venues that were not built for theatre—like clubs and basketball courts. There were a fair few disasters—injuries, truck breakdowns, illness, the lighting-board blowing up, blah blah blah. But the cast and crew always somehow managed a great show—even the injured ones pushing the pain barrier. And I think the audience reaction was worth the effort—noisy, responsive, having a bloody good time.

I drove out to join the guys for the second half of the tour. At the last show in the small town of Finley, more than 350 people crammed themselves into the high school hall. There's something especially exciting about performing for an audience who haven't had the chance to see much theatre. And there's something special about presenting the audience a story they can relate to, a story drawn from their experience.

The country tour of *Skate* was a stripped-back experience for me—with none of the theatre world trappings that can distort everyone's thinking. It was just about the basic stuff: actors telling the audience a story, trying to be honest in the face of people's lives and responsive to the passions of real life.

Anyway, that's why I feel so lucky to have been involved in this project—to work on a new full-length play for young audiences with such a great bunch of people. I owe huge thanks to Timothy Jones, David Berthold, atyp, the people of Deniliquin and the cast and crew of this production.

Sydney
January 2004

Skate was first produced by the Australian Theatre for Young People (atyp) at The Wharf, Walsh Bay, Sydney, on 12 April 2003 with the following cast:

ZAC	Richard Kessell
GAIL	Felicity Ward
AMY	Shannon Cranko
COREY	Blake Bowden
LAUREN	Elisha Oliver
JT	Jarryd Kirwan
TRAVIS	Mike Hamer
MITCHELL	Beejan Olfat
RILEY	Jonathan Latham
STELLA	Tessa de Josselin
RAY STONE	Anthony Gooley
JYSSYNTAH / TRISHA	Jessica Tuckwell
MARISSA / ALEXAKIS	Alex Vaughan
MATT / DENNIS	Robert Scurry

Directed by Timothy Jones
Design, Simon Greer
Lighting Design, Damien Cooper
Sound Design, Daniel Krass
Assistant Director, Amy Hardingham
Skate Choreographer, Al Foster

CHARACTERS

ZAC, 16

GAIL, 34, Zac's mum

AMY, 12, Zac's little sister, a skater

COREY, 16

LAUREN, 16

JT, 16, a clown, goofy, annoying but likeable

TRAVIS, 16, a wild boy, likes to hang with older bad guys

MITCHELL, 16, know-all enthusiast who never has a go himself

RILEY, 12, unstoppable, optimistic, idolises Zac

STELLA, 15, a capable girl skater, physically confident, unflappable

RAY STONE, local councillor and real estate agent

JYSSYNTAH, 15, pretty, flirty, ruthless

TRISHA, 34, Corey's mum

MARISSA, Jyssyntah's satellite, giggly, a bit dim, good-hearted

ALEXAKIS, police constable

MATT, 17

DENNIS, journalist

SCENE ONE

A pack of kids, some on skateboards, some on BMXs, swarms across the stage. They form an unruly chorus—sweeping us in and out of scenes, offering commentary. They are also part of the drama as individual characters.

This pack of kids can include, at various times, AMY, STELLA, MITCHELL, JT, TRAVIS *and* RILEY.

JYSSYNTAH *and* MARISSA *hang around the skaters but never skate.*

The pack takes over the skateable facade of the Town Hall including the steps and they've maybe constructed some makeshift skating ramps out of whatever junk they can find. They skate, ride bikes, sit on the edge dangling legs.

JT: The whole thing started last year—

TRAVIS: Way before then, retard.

RILEY: Yeah, what about the time before—?

JT: Okay, okay, but—

MITCHELL: Actually, you'd really have to go right back to the late 80s when—

JT: Whatever! We gotta pick one spot to start the story.

RILEY: Yeah, fair enough.

JT: Thank you. Now you made me forget what I was saying, deadheads.

STELLA: We skate around the Town Hall steps because we can't—

JT: Because there's nowhere else to skate in Narragindi—

TRAVIS: In this shitbox town.

ZAC *enters, nodding hello to a few people.*

JT: That's Zac.

JYSSYNTAH: Zac Marlowe.

RILEY: Zac's one of the most popular guys in the whole of Narragindi High.

JT: Oh, but he's not up himself or anything.

JYSSYNTAH: Zac's one of the only guys in Year Ten who is not a total retard—

MITCHELL: And he never bags anyone out.

TRAVIS: He's just a cool guy.

MARISSA: Don't you reckon Zac always looks like he's thinking something really deep?

JYSSYNTAH *rolls her eyes and groans at* MARISSA.

JT: [*joking to* TRAVIS] Zac's such a deep guy. Not like us, mate.

RILEY: Zac's one of the best skaters in Narra.

MITCHELL: What about Luke Macintosh?

AMY: He doesn't even live here anymore.

JT: What about me?

JT *goes for a trick and does an exaggerated slapstick fall.*

TRAVIS: JT—I worked out why you do all those spazzo falls.

JT: That's classic comic timing, mate.

TRAVIS: No, mate, you make a big funny-ha-ha deal out of it to cover for the fact that you can't skate for shit.

Whoops of laughter from the others.

TRAVIS: Stella knows I'm right, doncha Stella?

STELLA: I'm not saying anything.

JT: You are so totally dead, Travis.

JT *goes after* TRAVIS *but both laugh and end up flopped on their backs on the concrete. As the others skate around them, they both twist to get out of the way, squawking.*

COREY *enters with his board and for a moment stands apart while the others tell us about him.*

COREY:	G'day.
STELLA:	[*to the audience*] That's Corey.
MITCHELL:	His surname's Matthews.
JYSSYNTAH:	Matthews have always been the lowlife trash in Narragindi.

The kids take on mock-adult roles, superior, outraged, sly, as appropriate.

JT:	They live in a tin humpy.
TRAVIS:	Live like animals.
STELLA:	What about that disgusting display outside the Imperial Hotel? The Matthews woman—
JT:	In a catfight with her latest defacto. Drunk of course.
MITCHELL:	And the foul language.
STELLA:	You could see he's been hitting her again.
JYSSYNTAH:	Going back three generations, Matthews have been trash—
STELLA:	Dole bludgers.
JT:	Drunks.
TRAVIS:	Drug dealers.
MITCHELL:	Criminals.

Back to being themselves again:

TRAVIS:	When Corey first come back to Narra—
STELLA:	He'd been with a foster family in Wiley—
TRAVIS:	Whatever. I'm doing this bit, orright? He come to Narra High halfway through Year Seven.

JYSSYNTAH: Everyone knew he was a Matthews straight off.

MITCHELL: Some of the teachers—

TRAVIS: The really old ones.

STELLA: They used to teach Corey's mum and his uncles.

MITCHELL: One of his uncles got stabbed to death in jail. Stabbed with a screwdriver.

TRAVIS: It was a boxcutter, moron.

JYSSYNTAH: His other uncle's in jail too. Still alive but.

JT: The point is, some teachers picked on Corey. Like—'Oh, he's a Matthews so he must be a ratbag.'

TRAVIS: And Corey, he'd just go quiet and put up with it.

COREY *goes over to join* ZAC. *The two of them hang for a moment, talking.*

STELLA: Zac sat next to him in home room.

MARISSA: On account of their names—'Marlowe', then 'Matthews'. Get it?

TRAVIS: Zac stood up for Corey with the teachers.

JT: He'd go: 'It's not fair for Corey to get in trouble because he didn't know the system at our school, Mrs Henderson.'

TRAVIS: What's that voice meant to be?

JT: Zac.

TRAVIS: That sucks. Nothing like him. Zac!

ZAC: What?

TRAVIS: Say something.

ZAC: About what?

MITCHELL: Anything.

ZAC: [*grinning*] Are you dropkicks gonna skate or just yack all day?

ZAC *starts skating.* COREY *stuffs a trick clumsily.*

COREY:	[*sending himself up*] Aww… check it out.
ZAC:	[*laughing*] Getting some big air.
RILEY:	Corey's a good guy.
TRAVIS:	Even laughs at JT's lame jokes.
JT:	Fuck off!

RAY STONE, *early forties, in a suit, approaches the Town Hall. He makes a big show of being forced to dodge the skaters, sighing grimly, as if they are about to knock him over. In fact the skaters keep clear of him.*

RAY:	I'm trying to get into the building.
TRAVIS:	Need a hand up the steps, do ya?
ZAC:	Travis. Shut up.
RAY:	Are you kids blind? What does the sign say?

He indicates the 'No Skating' sign.

| JT: | Oh sorry, sorry—you're right. We should skate at the skatepark—oh… but—gasp! Hang on a sec… there isn't a skatepark in this town! |

ZAC *laughs but signals to* JT—*cool it.*

RAY *inspects the damaged edges of the building or dismantles some of the skating junk.*

AMY:	[*to the audience*] Mr Ray Stone.
STELLA:	Councillor Stone.
JT:	Real estate agent.
MITCHELL:	A heavy on the council.
RAY:	Should I send a bill to your parents for the damage you kids do here?

No response.

| RAY: | And what about the medical bills for the elderly people you knock over? Eh? |

The kids don't skate, they just hang.

TRAVIS: [*to the audience*] He's always had in it for the skaters.

STELLA: Him and a few old guys on the council went schizo about the campaign to get a skatepark.

The kids adopt the tone of grumpy old councillors:

JT: [*as a deaf old guy*] What are they after? A snakepark? We don't want snakes in Narragindi! What? A skatepark? Never heard of such a thing!

MITCHELL: We got by without a skatepark when we were kids.

AMY: It'd be a shocking waste of public money.

RILEY: Skateboarding is a passing fad.

STELLA: The thing would never get used. It'd be a white elephant in the middle of town.

JT: [*as a half-blind old guy*] Covered in graffiti! What does that graffiti there say? Something disgusting, I'll wager. Where are my glasses?

JYSSYNTAH: Everyone knows those skateparks attract youth gangs.

TRAVIS: Drug dealing.

RILEY: Foul language.

MITCHELL: And the ridiculous clothes they wear! Haven't those boys heard of belts?

JT: [*as an addled old guy*] The Narragindi Shire Council says no to—what is it again? Oh yes… No to the skatepark proposal!

A volley of grumpy 'no's from the chorus.

RAY: Any of you kids know anything about those damaged seats in Rotary Park?

A few half-hearted 'no's.

JT: [*aside, to the audience*] Anything happens within

a one-k radius of the skaters, it's automatically our fault.

TRAVIS: Dickhead.

RAY: [*challenging* TRAVIS] Something you wanted to say?

TRAVIS *glares at* RAY. ZAC *steps forward to block the eyeline.*

ZAC: He didn't say anything.

RAY: You can't skate here. Simple as that. Clear off.

RAY *goes inside.*

ZAC: [*to* TRAVIS] You can't win against guys like him. So don't take him on.

JT: Yeah, but Zac—come on—

ZAC *zooms straight down the curve on his board. He'd rather skate than talk about it. The older kids resume skating but the younger ones are apprehensive.*

ZAC: Hey, Riley—want me to show you how to do a nose-slide?

RILEY: [*indicating* RAY] But didn't he say—?

ZAC: Don't worry about it, mate.

RILEY: What about the sign?

ZAC: Are we hurting anyone?

MARISSA: [*trying to be helpful*] There was that lady at Easter who got knocked over.

ZAC: Yeah. Okay. [*Pointedly to* JT] If we're careful and don't skate like headcase losers—do we hurt anyone?

RILEY: Guess not.

ZAC: So we skate until they make us stop. So wanna have a go at a nose-slide?

RILEY: Yeah.

ZAC: Hey, Corey!

COREY *and* ZAC *teach* RILEY *how to do a nose-slide (or whatever trick seems appropriate).* RILEY *mucks it up a few times but the older boys keep working at it, patiently.*

Meanwhile MITCHELL *pulls a skating magazine out of his backpack.*

JT:	Is that the newest one? Give us a look.
MITCHELL:	See Tom Wheatley—that pro from Brisbane—
JT:	He got a massive sponsorship deal. That dude is living in luxury.
TRAVIS:	Wheatley's so gay.
JT:	Nah, he's a good skater. Kicks arse over Zac and Matt put together.
TRAVIS:	What can he do?
JT:	Front of the board right up, kisses it, lands it

From left: Mike Hamer as Travis, Beejan Olfat as Mitchell and Jarryd Kirwan as JT in the 2003 atyp production. (Photo: Phil Sheather)

perfect.

MITCHELL: Wheatley's riding exactly what I want. Exactly. See? [*Brandname*] deck, [*brandname*] trucks, [*brandname*] wheels.

STELLA: Excellent set-up.

JT: Yeah, sick. If you had to choose between your mother and your board, what would you choose?

TRAVIS: Board. No question.

JT: What about between your board and your girlfriend?

JYSSYNTAH *snorts and rolls her eyes, making* MARISSA *giggle.*

JT: [*meaning* MARISSA] I think your friend's got some kind of problem, Jyssyntah.

JYSSYNTAH: You retards are so kidding yourselves. You'd never be able to get a girlfriend anyway.

JT: You got something to say, Stella?

STELLA: [*grinning and skating off*] I'm not saying anything.

JYSSYNTAH *notices* LAUREN *nearby, holding a video camera. She's watching, especially* ZAC *and* COREY *helping* RILEY.

JYSSYNTAH: What's she doing here?

MARISSA: [*to the audience*] Lauren. She's in Year Ten like me and Zac and Travis and them.

LAUREN: Hi guys.

Muttered hellos. ZAC *is too busy skating but* COREY *is distracted by* LAUREN's *arrival.*

JT: What's the video camera in aid of?

LAUREN: I was wondering if you guys'd mind if I did some videoing of you skating.

TRAVIS: How much?

LAUREN:	Sorry?
TRAVIS:	How much do we get paid?
LAUREN:	Oh sorry… nothing—I—
STELLA:	He's just taking the piss. What's it for?
LAUREN:	There's this video competition I want to enter—
MITCHELL:	On skateboarding?
LAUREN:	It has to be on some aspect of youth activity.
JT:	Youth! That's us, Travis. I reckon we're 'youths'!

There's ad lib hooting about 'youth', saying the word over and over in silly voices. LAUREN *laughs.*

LAUREN:	Yeah well, it's pretty lame, I know. I didn't make up the idea for the competition.
MITCHELL:	What do you win?
LAUREN:	A whole lot of video gear.
JT:	Mad.
STELLA:	Why do skating but?
LAUREN:	Skating looks good on video. Better than a video of girls sitting around painting their nails, bitching about each other.

JYSSYNTAH *does a catty 'ooh', but* STELLA *nods—fair enough.*

JT:	Want us to do tricks for ya? For the movie? We can.
LAUREN:	Sure. That'd be great.
MITCHELL:	Oi, Zac! [*To* LAUREN] Zac's the best skater here.
ZAC:	What?
MITCHELL:	Do some tricks so Lauren can film it.

ZAC *shrugs and very slowly goes over to pick up his board.* COREY *waves hello to* LAUREN *and throws himself into a run—showing off for her.* LAUREN *videos the skaters.*

JT:	Awesome run, Corey.

MITCHELL:	Want me to explain the tricks Corey's doing?
LAUREN:	But don't you want to skate too?

Spluttering laughter from JYSSYNTAH, JT *and* TRAVIS.

JT:	Mitchell has a big mouth about skating.
TRAVIS:	Reads the mags, watches the videos, wears the clothes, talks his fucking head off about skating.
JYSSYNTAH:	But he doesn't do it.

MITCHELL *is used to this teasing.*

MITCHELL:	I happen to be waiting until I get the board I want. I'm not going to waste my time skating with crap equipment like you guys.

Hooting and guffaws in response.

LAUREN:	[*to* JYSSYNTAH *and* MARISSA] And what about you?
JT:	Don't think their legs work.
TRAVIS:	They just hang around hoping Matt'll turn up.
JT:	[*orgasmic*] Ooh, Matt. Oh, oh, oh Matt.

RILEY *and* AMY *join in the panting oohs and ahs, giggling.*

JYSSYNTAH:	Well, I wouldn't waste my breath on pimply retards like you guys.

ZAC *squats on the ground, tightening something on his board.*

COREY:	Do some more tricks for Lauren so her video turns out excellent.
ZAC:	She doesn't want to hang round here. She hates skaters.
COREY:	[*shrugging*] She's here. She's all right.
ZAC:	Too up-herself for mine.
COREY:	You reckon? I was in sick bay with her one time. She burnt her hand with acid in Science and I was crook from a dodgy hotdog. We talked a bit—in between me chucking my guts up.

ZAC: Mmm, romantic.

COREY: She talked to me. She was nice.

ZAC *is unconvinced.*

MATT *arrives.* JYSSYNTAH *goes into a full-on mating ritual.*

MATT: G'day.

JT: You gonna have a session? We're on camera.

MATT *checks out* LAUREN, *nods g'day to her.*

MATT: I've come straight from work. Don't have my
            board.

COREY: Have a lend of mine.

MATT: Ta.

MATT *uses* COREY'*s board to do a few runs. He and* ZAC *respect each other, skate together, chatting in between.*

JYSSYNTAH *and* MARISSA *slide along to be near one of* MATT'*s landing spots. Ad lib flirty chatter—'nice shirt', 'been at work?', 'that was amazing', etc.*

COREY *watches* LAUREN, *smitten, but too shy to approach her.*

ZAC *flies off the ramp at speed and* LAUREN, *filming him, has to jump out of the way.* ZAC *crouches to adjust something on his board.*

LAUREN: Do you mind me videoing you?

ZAC: Can't stop you.

LAUREN: I'll dub off a copy for you guys when it's finished.

ZAC: Whatever.

LAUREN: Is that all you can say? 'Whatever'?

ZAC: You were wanting a few lines of poetry?

LAUREN: Oh, so you graduated from Charm School with
            honours, did you Zac?

ZAC: I'm just a skater. What can you expect?

LAUREN: Excuse me. You don't know what I think.

ZAC: Whatever.

He skates off.

LAUREN: [*to* JYSSYTNTAH] So up himself. Have you seen him sloping around school seething—like something's biting his bum? The Angry Young Man act is so tedious.

JYSSYNTAH: Don't ask me. I don't understand half the things you say.

Annoyed by LAUREN *and miffed that* MATT *is ignoring her,* JYSSYNTAH *flounces off, flicking her head for* MARISSA *to follow.*

JYSSYNTAH: This is boring. Let's go.

MARISSA: Oh, but I wanna watch the—

JYSSYNTAH: I said let's go, Marissa.

Faced with JYSSYNTAH*'s sharp look,* MARISSA *jumps up obediently and follows her offstage.*

RILEY *does a really good trick.*

ZAC: Good one, Riley.

COREY: Yeah, heaps good.

LAUREN *films* STELLA *who's working on a difficult trick.*

MITCHELL: You know why you can't get that trick to work?

STELLA *makes a big show of peering around and trying to clear her ears.*

STELLA: What's that farting noise? It's like there's some wannabe skater telling me what to do…

MITCHELL: You got your feet too far forward for a frontside nosegrind.

STELLA: Like you'd know. The Expert.

MITCHELL: I saw Harley Preston do one on a video. He has his feet further back.

STELLA *ignores him, tries again. This time the trick works.*

_____MITCHELL: See?

STELLA *roars and chucks something at him, but she's grinning. He laughs and shields himself with the magazine.*

_____JT: Hey, Riley, have a go at grinding down those steps.

RILEY *shakes his head, daunted.*

_____JT: Not scared are ya, little dude?

JT *leaps around* RILEY, *being a scary monster.*

_____ZAC: Leave him alone, JT. You didn't do stuff like that when you were only—How old are you, Riley?

_____RILEY: Twelve.

_____ZAC: Don't worry about this clown, okay Riley. He still can't do any decent tricks. Can you, JT?

JT *prepares to do a trick with a great flourish. Then he does a spectacular fall, sprawling at* RILEY's *feet, making him giggle.*

TRAVIS, STELLA *and* MITCHELL *are huddled around the camera, watching some footage on replay.*

_____MITCHELL: Corey—there's you doing a sick indie grab. Come and look.

_____LAUREN: I'll rewind it to that bit.

COREY *shyly comes over and stands close beside* LAUREN *so he can see the footage.*

_____LAUREN: That's you. Looks good, eh.

_____COREY: Hey… yeah.

_____LAUREN: Thanks for helping me out with this stuff.

_____COREY: Oh well…

_____LAUREN: Look at this bit.

She focuses on the screen. COREY *sneaks sideways looks at her.*

_____LAUREN: Eaten any rank hotdogs lately?

Elisha Oliver as Lauren and Blake Bowden as Corey in the 2003 atyp production. (Photo: Phil Sheather)

COREY: Oh… no. Luckily. How's your hand? I mean, is it—you know…?

LAUREN: [*conspiratorially*] It was never that bad. I just wanted an excuse to get out of Cleveland's Science class. Don't dob me in.

She smiles at COREY. *He is totally smitten now.*

JT *does a loud siren sound effect.*

JT: Cop alert! Cop alert!

*A young female police officer approaches—*CONSTABLE ALEXAKIS. *She is sympathetic but firm.*

ALEXAKIS: G'day, guys.

Muttered hellos. They don't mind her.

ALEXAKIS: Have to ask you to stop skating here.

TRAVIS: That maggot Ray Stone rung you guys up, I bet.

ALEXAKIS: Doesn't matter, Travis. There's the sign. It's my job to ask you to stop.

JT: That's cool. Just tell us where else we can skate.

ALEXAKIS: Guys, I don't think it's fair. But that's how it is for now.

TRAVIS: For fucking ever.

The skaters collect up their gear to leave.

ALEXAKIS: Hi, Corey. How's things?

COREY *shrinks, head down and quiet when the cop's around.*

COREY: Orright.

A lairy car horn sounds. TRAVIS *signals towards the car—'wait for me'—and runs off.*

TRAVIS: My brother. I'm out of here.

ALEXAKIS: Travis, go easy. Use your brain more than your brother does, eh.

MATT *hands* COREY *back his board.*

> MATT: Thanks for the lend. All I need now's a car so I can drive out of this useless bloody town.

MATT *signals goodbye to* ZAC *and goes.*

All the kids have stopped skating except ZAC *who swoops back and forth, joyless and defiant.*

> ALEXAKIS: Zac. Come on. Don't be silly.

He keeps skating.

> ALEXAKIS: Stop now or I'll have to confiscate your board. You know that.

She steps forward to meet him on the next swoop.

> ALEXAKIS: Give me the board.

ZAC *steps off the board at speed, letting it fly out behind him.* MATT *picks up the board.*

> ALEXAKIS: Can you promise me you'll stop skating here if I give you back the board?
> ZAC: No.
> ALEXAKIS: Then I'll have to confiscate it.

Reluctantly ALEXAKIS *takes the board and goes.*

> JT: [*yelling after her*] Thank you, officer! We feel much safer in our community now with those dreadful skaters off the streets!

ZAC *packs up his gear to leave.*

> LAUREN: What did that prove? That little macho display. Now you can't skate anyway.

ZAC *doesn't answer.*

> LAUREN: I mean, if you want to go in for the big symbolic stand, why don't you push for a skatepark or whatever?

ZAC *glares at her and walks off.*

LAUREN: Charming. I love the articulate response to my question.

COREY: Zac gets the shits because—look, people tried to get us a skatepark and it never happened. Hey, Zac.

COREY *runs after him.*

MITCHELL: [*to the audience*] Two and half years Zac and the others went flat out on the skatepark campaign—

JT: Nuh, three years.

MITCHELL: Okay, three years. Zac and—

JT: Atchally it was more than three years.

MITCHELL: It was a long fucking time, okay? Zac—

AMY: And me.

RILEY: And older kids who've left town now.

AMY: Don't forget my mum.

STELLA: Yeah, Zac's mum helped.

JT: They got donations.

MITCHELL: They did proper designs and engineer reports and all that.

STELLA: Sat through hours of council meetings—

JT: So boring you'd rather eat your own head off.

RILEY: Worked their guts out.

JT: Skatepark never happened but.

LAUREN: I'm sure there's a way you could get—My uncle's on the council. I could ask him what the problem is.

MITCHELL: Who's your uncle?

LAUREN: Ray Stone.

Hoots and guffaws.

LAUREN: What?

JT: What town you been living in, girlie?

STELLA: Uncle Ray is the problem with the skatepark. One of them anyway.

LAUREN: You're so paranoid. There's no conspiracy. I mean, the council aren't evil. Put a reasonable case to them and they'll—

JT: And they'll come up with excuses and stall for years until everyone—

He falls into mock sleep with loud snoring.

MITCHELL: Until everyone gets the shits with it and gives up.

STELLA: Which is exactly what happened to Zac.

The kids wander off.

LAUREN: [*calling after* AMY] So does your brother get his board back or what?

AMY: If Mum goes down the police station. Again.

SCENE TWO

The police station.

GAIL *walks in with* ZAC *trailing sullenly behind. She wears a chemist shop uniform.*

ALEXAKIS: How are you, Gail?

GAIL: [*wearily cheerful*] Overworked, disappointed by life, driven mental by my kids—y'know, great.

ALEXAKIS: Sorry about the skateboard business.

GAIL: You have to do it. Since we live in Grumpsville, run by nasty old grumps who grew up and forgot they were ever kids. People who think—

ZAC: [*embarrassed, please stop*] Mum…

GAIL:	I recommend you keep a low profile, mate. Seeing as you made me drag myself down here yet again.
ALEXAKIS:	I'll finish up in here and then dig out the board for you.
GAIL:	Ta.

ALEXAKIS *goes off.*

GAIL:	This is the last time, Zac. Next time you can pay the damn fine.
ZAC:	Cool by me. Only I'll have to leave school and get a job to earn the money to pay the damn fines.
GAIL:	Dream on. There's no way—
ZAC:	Once I finish Year Ten, you can't make me stay at school. That was the deal.
GAIL:	Nup. I can't make you. But you know—
ZAC:	[*mimicking her*] 'Work hard and you'll get the benefit.' I worked hard at school and what did it get me?
GAIL:	Bloody good results until you decided to slack off—
ZAC:	You work hard. Where's it get you? Stuck at ChemistZone earning ripoff money, stuck in this shithole town with no life except the occasional sleazoid guy trying to crack onto you in the bowling club—
GAIL:	Okay, Zac, you made your point.
ZAC:	I'm getting out of Narra soon as—
GAIL:	Good. I hope you get out. Stay on at school and then you'll have options for when—
ZAC:	Oh yeah, like doing a project on the Aztecs is really gonna help my life.

GAIL: Don't insult my intelligence and yours, Zac—

ZAC: That school sucks. Whole system's totally unfair. So why bother?

GAIL: You bother because—

They fall silent when TRISHA BEGGS *emerges from inside the station, followed by* ALEXAKIS. TRISHA *is the same age as* GAIL *but looks older, her face bruised and split from a recent bashing. She lurches between waspish aggression and whiney friendliness.*

GAIL: Hi Trisha.

ALEXAKIS: If you could sign these, Trisha— [*To* GAIL] Be with you in one sec.

TRISHA *signs documents on the counter.*

ALEXAKIS: If you decide to make a complaint against Warren for the… [*indicating the facial injuries*] … we can fill out—

TRISHA: Nuh.

ALEXAKIS: Well, if you change your mind—

TRISHA: I said no, all-fucking-right? I just wanna get Warren's car released and then I'm out of here.

TRISHA *rolls her eyes to* GAIL—*appealing for sympathy.*

GAIL: How's Corey going?

TRISHA: You tell me. My son practically lives at your place.

GAIL: Well… you know, we like having him round.

TRISHA: Yeah… look, I know.

GAIL: Corey's been missing a bit of school. Hard if he gets behind in Year Ten—

TRISHA: Oh right, you wanna have a go at me too like every other mongrel in this town, do ya?

GAIL: No. Sorry. I was just—

TRISHA: Yeah, well, you keep your sticky fucking beak out of my family's business, orright?

_____GAIL: Okay.

ALEXAKIS *hands* GAIL *the skateboard.*

_____GAIL: Thanks.

GAIL *and* ZAC *start to leave.* TRISHA *grabs* GAIL*'s arm.*

_____TRISHA: Look, Gail, I'm—y'know… I know you look after
                  Corey when things—when I need to get things
                  sorted out and—anyway, I know you look out
                  for him.

_____GAIL: He's a good kid, Trisha.

GAIL *and* ZAC *exit.*

*The skating pack comes through, taking us from the police station.
While the pack tell us about Warren Beggs, we see* TRISHA *leave
the police station and walk over to where* COREY *is waiting. He's
talking to her (unheard), concerned about her split face, but she
shrugs him off.*

_____JT: Corey's stepdad—

_____STELLA: Warren Beggs.

_____JT: —he's a deadset scary guy.

_____MITCHELL: People reckon he's a big drug dealer.

_____STELLA: He's definitely been in jail a few times.

_____JT: Dad crosses the street if he sees him. He goes
              'Warren Beggs is a hard man.'

_____MITCHELL: [*as a parent*] 'A truly nasty piece of work.'

TRISHA *goes offstage, leaving* COREY *alone in the street.*

_____STELLA: Warren Beggs hates Corey.

_____TRAVIS: For no reason. Just hates his guts.

_____JT: Corey's not allowed to breathe around his
              stepdad.

_____MITCHELL: Everyone knows Corey's got a lot to put up with.

_____TRAVIS: When Corey's had a gutful of it—

JT: He grabs his board and goes round to Zac's.

TRAVIS: Yeah, bedsurfs for a couple of days—

STELLA: Till it's safe to go home.

The skaters deliver us to Zac's place as COREY *is heading there:*

SCENE THREE

Zac's place.

ZAC *mucks around doing flatland tricks.* AMY *is flopped out watching TV.* GAIL *flies around being a busy single mother.*

GAIL: Actually, I remember the Aztecs were pretty bloody interesting. Weren't they the ones who sacrificed people and made tequila out of cactuses? Something like that.

ZAC: Great. You go to school and learn about the fucking Aztecs.

GAIL: I'd love the chance to go to tech or uni or whatever and learn—

ZAC: So you keep saying. Well, I'm not stopping you.

GAIL *opens her mouth to argue back but gives up, hopeless.*

COREY: Hi.

ZAC *cheers up as soon as* COREY *arrives.*

GAIL: G'day, Corey. How are you?

COREY: Okay, thanks.

GAIL: How's your mum?

COREY: Oh, y'know…

GAIL *smiles, sympathetic.*

COREY: Oh, sorry—didn't realise you were about to have dinner—

GAIL: There's plenty. And stay the night if you want—might be easier, eh.

COREY: Oh. Ta. [*Whispering to* ZAC] Sure your mum isn't starting to mind me crashing here so much?

ZAC: No way. She likes you more than me. You big suck.

COREY *gives* ZAC *a get-fucked shove and* ZAC *does a spectacular fall as if he's been thumped hard.*

ZAC: That's right, isn't it Mum? You like Corey bludging round here.

GAIL: God, yes. When you're here, 'It' [*meaning* ZAC] actually smiles. Makes a nice change from the turbo-charged sulking we usually get.

GAIL *and* COREY *exchange a grin at* ZAC's *expense.*

ZAC: I love you too, Mum.

ZAC *and* GAIL *do kissing and pouty 'I love you's, sarcastic but good-natured underneath.*

ZAC: [*to* COREY] Let's go before she runs off at the mouth again. [*To* GAIL] I'll set the mattresses up in the sleepout, eh.

GAIL: Sure. Hey, Corey, if you want to have a skate in Glenthorpe in the morning, I'm driving down—

ZAC: You going to Glen?

GAIL: To get photos of their skatepark for a new campaign.

ZAC: You starting a new campaign? Give it a rest, Mum. Let it die.

GAIL: I'm not asking you to help anymore.

ZAC: Why keep bashing your head against a brick wall? What are you trying to prove?

GAIL: Whose idea was the skatepark campaign in the

first place?

ZAC: When I was a stupid little kid who didn't realise how fucked everything is.

AMY: Shut up and don't be a dickhead to Mum.

GAIL: Thank you, Amy, and watch your mouth. There might be a new possibility. I sent off for this.

She slaps down a brightly printed brochure. AMY *grabs it and reads eagerly.*

GAIL: OzYouth Grants. Some new government thing where they're giving money to—

AMY: [*brandishing the brochure*] To skateparks and that!

ZAC: As if.

GAIL: Well, sure, we have to raise a quarter of the money—

AMY: Then OzYouth give us the rest—that's what it says. This is so excellent.

GAIL: We need a presentation—photos and whatever —to show people, so they'll make donations.

ZAC: Believe it when I see it.

GAIL *is determined not to bite at his cynicism.*

GAIL: Anyway. If you guys want to have a skate in Glen, there's room in the car.

COREY: That'd be cool. [*To* ZAC] You know, Lauren's making that movie about skating—what do you reckon, Zac?

ZAC: About what?

COREY: [*to* GAIL] We could ask Lauren to come and videotape the skatepark in Glen. Would that be a good idea?

GAIL: Great idea. I'll give her a call.

ZAC: That's a bad, bad idea. Lauren? Shithouse idea.

GAIL: And is anyone asking you? You don't want to be part of the campaign, fine—

ZAC: Yeah, whatever. None of my business.

COREY: But you're gonna come to Glen for a skate.

ZAC: Any chance for a session at a decent park.

SCENE FOUR

The pack of skaters sweeps across stage to create a park in Glenthorpe. We can see the edge of one of the skateramps, with the rest of the skatepark suggested offstage.

MITCHELL: Takes an hour and a half on the bus from Narra to Glenthorpe.

JYSSYNTAH: An hour if you can bludge a lift off your parents or someone.

STELLA: Forty-five minutes if Travis's speedfreak brother is driving.

JT: [*as a mock tour guide*] Ladies and gents, you are entering scenic Glenthorpe! Tidy Town runner-up in 1973!

TRAVIS: Glen sucks.

JYSSYNTAH: They've got movies.

TRAVIS: Their skatepark is so gay.

MITCHELL: Yeah, only one squitchy flatbank and the funbox is shitful.

STELLA: At least they've got a skatepark.

RILEY: Ours'd be better.

MITCHELL: If we ever get one.

JT: Ah, too many rollerbladers in Glen.

Maybe a rollerblader comes through to be met with abuse:

STELLA:	Rollerbladers think they're better than us.
TRAVIS:	Wankers.
STELLA:	Pizzacutters.
JT:	Fruitbooters.
TRAVIS:	Rollerpoofs.
JT:	Masturbladers.

The group skates off, laughing, as ZAC, COREY, AMY, LAUREN *and* GAIL *arrive at the park.*

COREY *is smitten with* LAUREN *but shy around her.*

LAUREN *films* ZAC *and* AMY *skating while* GAIL *takes still photos. (They mostly skate offstage, occasionally appearing on the section of ramp we can see.)*

GAIL:	Once we get these photos and budgets and the other stuff together, we need some kids to present it—do a speech and explain why the skatepark would be—
COREY:	But can't you talk to people and explain why—?
GAIL:	It can't be an adult.
COREY:	Right, I get you. But I'm not—
LAUREN:	It's a reasonable proposal. Everyone will see that.
GAIL:	Well, probably not. The grumps've pretty much worn me down. This'll be my last bash at it.
COREY:	Sorry… I don't think a guy like me can be much help…
GAIL:	'Course you can.

GAIL *takes a snap of him and* COREY *grins, embarrassed.*

ZAC:	[*to* LAUREN] You wanna watch out. That's a Matthews you've been talking to.
LAUREN:	What? What shite is coming out of your mouth now?
ZAC:	I'm just pointing out—

LAUREN: No, you're just being a prize creep. You accuse me of thinking this or that without even knowing me.

ZAC *shrugs and skates off.*

COREY: Zac gets in a bad mood about the skatepark stuff.

LAUREN: I'm sorry, I know he's your friend, but he is such a—

She growls, annoyed.

COREY: Zac stuck up for me at school. Didn't have to, but he did.

LAUREN: That's great, but—

COREY: And he's deadset clever too.

LAUREN: Yeah?

COREY: Smarter than me by a million per cent.

LAUREN: Don't put yourself down.

COREY: Why bother doing it myself when everybody else'll do it for me?

LAUREN: Don't talk like that. What do you want to do when you finish school?

COREY: Oh… judging by the family form guide, jail and the dole.

LAUREN: Come on, Corey, don't say—

COREY: What about you?

LAUREN: Well, I've got a five-year plan. You've gotta keep paddling hard in a town like Narra so you don't just sink into the ooze. First, get the best HSC I can, keep working on videos until I get into one of the top film schools. I'm not naïve. It's not going to be easy. And I know—

COREY *is staring at her—totally smitten.*

LAUREN: [*laughing*] What? You think I'm a wanker.

COREY:	No way.
LAUREN:	What would you do if you could do anything in the world?
COREY:	What are you, a career guidance counsellor?
LAUREN:	I want an answer.
COREY:	Ohh… few times I thought, 'be good to get an apprenticeship', but who in Narra'd give me an apprenticeship? No one. Sometimes I imagine if Zac started up his own skating and BMX magazine—like he says sometimes—and I'd work on it for him. I'd like that. I'd love it.
LAUREN:	That's possible. Definitely.
COREY:	Get some money together. Buy Mum a house.
LAUREN:	And you could maybe—

From left to right (in background): Mike Hamer as Travis, Beejan Olfat as Mitchell, Jonathan Latham as Riley; (foreground) Elisha Oliver as Lauren and Blake Bowden as Corey in the 2003 atyp production. (Photo: Phil Sheather)

COREY: But right now, I gotta make sure my mum's okay and that. So not much point thinking about it—y'know, the future.

COREY *closes down, upset.* LAUREN *isn't sure what to say. She watches him spin his skateboard on the ground.*

LAUREN: How did you get your deck?

COREY: One time I was living with this foster family. And DOCS bought a bike or a board for all the foster kids in Narra and Wiley Creek that Christmas-time. So I was pretty lucky with the timing.

LAUREN: Skaters get ripped off with all that expensive gear. Fashion victims, I reckon.

COREY: Prob'ly. One time when my mum was in hospital—

LAUREN: Was she sick or—?

COREY *shrugs and nods vaguely.*

COREY: Thing is, I was staying at Zac's and anyway Gail, she came back from Glen with this [*brandname*] shirt she bought for me. Reckoned she got it on some amazing special, but—

LAUREN: But you reckon she paid full price.

COREY: You always do for that gear.

LAUREN: Shit, it's not like she's rolling in dough.

COREY: And she's got her own kids to buy stuff for and everything. I wore that shirt every single day for the holidays and every single night Gail washed it out for me because I didn't have any other good gear.

LAUREN: [*meaning the one he's wearing*] Is that it?

COREY: Oh no. Maybe washing it so much made it get thinned out and crappy quicker. Because one time my stepdad grabbed a fistful of the front and I kind of yanked away from him and the shirt got ripped. You probably think I'm a headcase—going on about a t-shirt—

    LAUREN: No, I don't. I get what you mean—

ZAC *blasts off the ramp on his board, smashing into* COREY *and* LAUREN.

    ZAC: Whoops! Sorry!

LAUREN *scrambles to protect her video camera, annoyed.* COREY *laughs and chases* ZAC *away.*

    COREY: Get out of it, you feral idiot!

    LAUREN: [*walking away*] I'll edit this video footage into a proper sequence.

LAUREN, GAIL *and* AMY *exit as the skating pack kids dismantle Glenthorpe Park. Meanwhile* ZAC *and* COREY *wander downstage together (back to Narragindi).*

SCENE FIVE

Zac's room.

ZAC *unpacks his stuff from the Glenthorpe trip while* COREY *pokes around the room.*

    ZAC: What are you snooping around my room for?

    COREY: You still got that model thingo? It was under—

    ZAC: Still under the bed, yeah.

COREY *pulls out a small scale model of a skatepark, built onto a square of chipboard. He blows the dust off it.*

    COREY: How long ago did you make this?

    ZAC: My twelfth birthday, I got this money from my nanna. Went to the hardware store and bought stuff to make it.

    COREY: It's like an exact scale model of the skatepark

we want, yeah?

ZAC: Yeah. I thought—I was only twelve, remember—I thought once people saw the model, they'd go: 'Oh right, Zac, we get you now. That looks great.'

COREY: Be great to show this to people in presentations and that... Would it be okay if I borrowed it just for—?

ZAC: Have it.

COREY: Don't give it to me. I don't want to wreck it.

ZAC: Not doing me any good getting festy under my bed. Keep it. It's yours now.

COREY: You sure?

ZAC: Sure.

COREY: You should get on the campaign. Be better at it than a dropkick like me.

ZAC: True.

COREY: Go on.

ZAC: Nah... it's your business if you wanna have a go, but—

COREY: People reckon we got a good chance this time. A heaps good chance.

ZAC: I'd hate to see you get all psyched and then—

COREY: And then the old bastards kill it dead. That's what you think'll happen.

ZAC: I know how lousy it felt, that's all.

ZAC *skates off.*

The pack of skaters watches COREY *holding the model with reverential care.*

MITCHELL: Corey carried that model with him everywhere, practically.

TRAVIS: He fuckin' loved that thing.

GAIL, AMY *and* RILEY *enter in busy mode, in the swing of the campaign.*

JT: [*a big announcement to the audience*] Those guys got cracking on the campaign to get us a skatepark in Narra.

GAIL *yacks on a phone, crossing names off a list.* AMY *and* RILEY *go around the audience collecting donations in buckets and selling raffle tickets.*

AMY: Do you want to buy a raffle ticket to help the skatepark campaign?

RILEY: Excellent prizes. First prize is a fantastic skateboard set-up.

GAIL: [*to* COREY] Presentation to the Apex Club on Friday night. To see if they'll make a donation.

COREY: Me? I'm not the one who should be—

COREY *stands there with the model, looking petrified.* LAUREN *enters, hands him a videotape and heads off.*

LAUREN: Here's the video. You can use it in the presentation.

COREY: But what do I say? I can't do this...

LAUREN: Well, have you written a speech?

COREY: Tried to. But I'm not—they won't listen to me—

LAUREN: Kids in this town deserve a fair go the same as everyone else, don't they?

COREY: Well—

LAUREN: I mean, skating is a legitimate youth activity and if the skatepark is properly set up, it won't cause all the problems people are stressing about. Actually, it'll solve problems because kids will have something fun to do and that's—

COREY: You do it.

LAUREN: Do what?

COREY: You do the speech. You're amazing.

LAUREN: Look, I'll help you write something and then you can—

COREY: No. I can't. Not like you. You do it. Please.

JT: That's how Lauren got roped into it.

LAUREN *turns, confronted with a microphone and a spotlight, addressing the audience as if they're the Apex members.*

LAUREN: So, as you can see, this skatepark is about giving a share of resources and a fair go to the youth of Narragindi.

COREY: And it would be, like, a great place for kids to meet up with their friends in the middle of town and—uh—

He freezes up with nerves. LAUREN *gives him a smile of encouragement.*

COREY: If you want to look at the plans and the model and—umm—ask any questions, you can. Thanks for listening to us.

STELLA: [*to the audience*] Lauren and Corey and Zac's mum and them worked their guts out.

COREY *and* LAUREN *take the model and the skatepark plans around the audience.* AMY *and* RILEY *continue selling tickets.* GAIL *is on the phone, dealing with papers, adding up figures on a calculator. We maybe see* ZAC *wheeling past on his skateboard, watching but not involved.*

MITCHELL: They did presentations to every club and organisation in town.

STELLA: They got a letter out of the council to say if we got the grant to pay for the skatepark, we could have the land.

TRAVIS: They flogged raffle tickets and scrounged donations from all over.

MITCHELL:	Did budgets and filled out fifteen million forms.
JT:	Wrote pages of blahblah about the skatepark to ask for the OzYouth grant.
STELLA:	And crossed their fingers.

The sequence ends with LAUREN *selling raffle tickets on the street.*

SCENE SIX

Town street.

LAUREN *approaches* RAY STONE *as he comes past with real estate advertising poster boards.*

LAUREN:	Uncle Ray. Don't suppose you want to buy a raffle ticket.
RAY:	No thank you, Lauren.
LAUREN:	I guess not, since you voted against every skatepark proposal in the last four years.
RAY:	You've been doing some background homework. Shame you're not putting effort into something more productive.
LAUREN:	Maybe if you look at the proposal—
RAY:	You think it's so simple. 'We want this skatepark so we should get it.' There are people—elderly, for example—who are frightened by the whole skating business. I have to look out for their interests too.
LAUREN:	But if people gave it a chance—
RAY:	I've seen skateparks in other towns. Built with good intentions. But those places turned into magnets for gangs and drug dealing. So ordinary people are afraid to go near—
LAUREN:	Come on, you can't blame skating for those

problems. And if our skatepark was in the middle of town, visible and safe, then—

RAY: I told your dad it's a shame you're wasting your time with this nonsense, Lauren.

LAUREN: Why won't you even listen to—?

RAY: What a shame. What a great shame.

LAUREN: You know what? I always thought if someone had a reasonable idea, then they'd get listened to at least. But I can't believe the negative junk that spins round in some people's brains—

RAY: I want this town to be a decent place—for everyone—which means making what I think are the right choices. One day you might have the maturity to understand that.

RAY *snatches up the advertising board and goes.* ZAC *has been observing their argument.*

ZAC: So it's working then.

LAUREN: What? Are you talking to me?

ZAC: You helping the skatepark campaign—oooh, Lauren the rebel girl.

LAUREN: Being a nauseating turd—that's your special gift, is it?

ZAC: Pissing off your family: that's why you got into this, isn't it?

LAUREN: Maybe a bit. To start with. But not now.

ZAC *and* LAUREN *shut up and stare as* COREY *and his mum* TRISHA *appear at the far end of the street.* TRISHA *stumbles, drunk and upset, incoherent.* COREY *steadies her, upset himself but trying to maintain calm. We see and hear enough to know that he's persuading her to go home.* ZAC *and* LAUREN *watch until* COREY *and* TRISHA *are out of sight.*

LAUREN: Is Corey all right? I mean, at home—

ZAC: It's none of your business.

LAUREN: Guess not. Look Zac, you—even though you're a total dick—I know you're a good friend of Corey's.

ZAC: He's a good guy.

LAUREN: I'm not arguing with you.

ZAC: I've never heard him say one nasty word about anyone even though people spew out massive piles of nasty words about him and his family. Corey just sticks to his friends and tries to do the right thing.

LAUREN: Hey, I like Corey too.

ZAC: Yeah, well, don't even think about mucking him round. He's got enough hassles as it is.

SCENE SEVEN

Pizza place.

The skating pack comes roaring onstage in a whooping frenzy. LAUREN, GAIL *and* COREY *are with them, all beaming and euphoric.*

RILEY: We got it!

AMY: We got it! We got the grant!

STELLA: Reached the target and OzYouth said yes.

JT: Yes—a big juicy grant to build the skatepark!

MITCHELL: The council said we could have the bit of the park if we got the OzYouth grant—thinking we'd never get the grant.

JT: But we did! Ha!

STELLA: So now the council's got no excuse.

MATT: Those council blokes'll be spewing about it.

TRAVIS: Who cares? We fuckin' won.

STELLA: A skatepark smack bang in the middle of town, opposite Memorial Park.

_____RILEY: Narra gets a skatepark!

_____JT: Party! Party!

*Whoops of triumph as they sweep across and set up a party in
the pizza place and courtyard.*

_____MITCHELL: Everyone got invited back to Stella's dad's pizza
                    place.

_____STELLA: Even bludgers who never helped get the
                    skatepark.

_____JT: Bludgers like me! Yes!

ZAC *gets scooped up and taken along to the party too.*

_____TRAVIS: Heaps good pizza at this place.

_____MITCHELL: But you have to go the extra cheese.

_____JT: Good point.

_____MATT: We pretty much took over the place for the night.

_____STELLA: Courtyard out the back, so there's plenty of room.

_____AMY: Stella's dad kept sliding pizzas out of the oven
                    and onto the tables.

_____MITCHELL: And he rigged the jukebox so you didn't need
                    coins to play songs.

_____JT: Mostly crap music but still, excellent.

*Pizza boxes and drink cans are chucked around as everyone gets
some.*

_____JT: We were all so stoked, we almost forgot about
                    the raffle.

_____STELLA: But on that exact day the raffle prizes arrived
                    from [*name of a skateshop*].

GAIL *and* AMY *carry on prizes—caps, t-shirts, etc. and first prize—an
elaborately displayed skateboard.*

_____RILEY: Far out... look at that.

_____MITCHELL: That is a great board. The perfect set-up.

_____GAIL: Let's draw first prize, eh.

AMY *holds up a bucket with the tickets in.* GAIL *makes a big barrel-girl show of fishing a ticket out.*

_____GAIL: Lucky winner is: E24. Who's got E24?

Kids scramble to find their tickets. Ad libs about not having it, disappointment, wondering who's got it.

_____STELLA: Mitchell? You okay?

MITCHELL *is frozen, ticket in hand.* RILEY *peers down to look.*

_____RILEY: E24! He's got it!

_____JT: Aha! Mitchie... isn't this... [*indicating the prize*] the exact set-up you've been waiting to get?

_____RILEY: So now you can skate!

_____JT: I think that's what Mitchell's packing shit about.

MITCHELL *stands holding the prize like a stunned mullet.*

_____STELLA: Mitchell. Come over here. I want to say something to you.

STELLA *beckons and* MITCHELL *follows her offstage.*

The skating pack moves beyond view offstage, into the restaurant itself. Music and sounds of the celebration spill out the doors into the courtyard where ZAC *wanders out with a slice of pizza.* COREY *comes out looking for him.*

_____COREY: Hiding out here, are ya?

_____ZAC: You were right and I was wrong.

_____COREY: Hey. It was your skatepark plan in the first place.

ZAC *shrugs dismissively at that idea.*

_____ZAC: Congratulations, mate.

_____COREY: Thanks.

_____ZAC: No. Really.

_____COREY: Thanks. Really.

ZAC *shoves him.* COREY *staggers sideways, laughing.*

       COREY: D'you see if Lauren went back inside?

ZAC *snorts dismissively.*

       COREY: Why do you hate her so much?

       ZAC: I don't hate her.

       COREY: I think she's an excellent person. Do you reckon she's—?

       ZAC: Up herself? Yep.

       COREY: No. Do you reckon she ever thinks—?

       ZAC: Ever thinks she's better than the rest of us? Yep.

       COREY: [*sick of it*] Zac.

       ZAC: Sorry, sorry.

       COREY: I like her.

       ZAC: Yeah, I know.

       COREY: No. I mean, like, really.

       ZAC: I know. Really.

       COREY: D'you reckon she'd ever…? I mean…

       ZAC: Oh, mate… be careful, you know. A girl like that? Who knows. Hate to see you get mangled.

       COREY: Yeah, like why would she be interested in me? As if.

       ZAC: For one thing, you're shockin' ugly.

       COREY: Bit scrawny.

       ZAC: Plus there's the smell.

       COREY: Thanks for setting me straight on me being a repulsive dog, mate.

       ZAC: You're welcome.

STELLA *and* MITCHELL *(stuffing his face with pizza) cross the courtyard.* STELLA *carries* MITCHELL*'s new skateboard, still in its fancy prize wrapping.*

       STELLA: Just try it. Out here on the flat.

MITCHELL, *mouth too full to speak, shakes his head emphatically.*

    COREY: You guys seen Lauren?

    STELLA: She's somewhere.

COREY *heads off to look for her.*

    STELLA: [*to* MITCHELL] Just have a little go. No one out here to see you.

MITCHELL *points to* ZAC.

    ZAC: I don't count.

    STELLA: He doesn't count. Roll forward and try a basic ollie. I learned right here in this courtyard.

    MITCHELL: I can do an ollie. I told you. I'm just waiting until I get—

    STELLA: Mitchell, you don't have to bullshit. It's just me—

    ZAC: And me.

    STELLA: And Zac. It's okay to admit you don't know how to—

    MITCHELL: Are you people deaf? Leave me alone.

MITCHELL *escapes and* STELLA *follows, badgering him.*

    STELLA: Come on, Mitchell, don't be such a girl.

GAIL *finds* ZAC *sitting out there alone.*

    GAIL: Hello, you. Getting away from the noise for a sec?

    ZAC: Just thinking about stuff.

    GAIL: Careful. Your brain might explode.

She grabs his head in a playful wrestle.

    GAIL: What stuff?

    ZAC: What 'what stuff'?

    GAIL: That you're thinking about.

    ZAC: Oh. Corey and that, I guess.

GAIL: Did he say things are really rancid for him at home?

ZAC: He doesn't talk about it.

GAIL: No. He's pretty happy tonight anyway.

ZAC: He's so stoked about the skatepark. Reckons it's the happiest he's ever been. [*As* COREY] 'Happiest by—'

GAIL: [*joining in as* COREY] '—by a million per cent.'

ZAC *and* GAIL *smile. They both love* COREY.

GAIL: Well, happy is good, isn't it?

ZAC: Yeah. It's excellent.

GAIL: But you still worry about him.

ZAC *shrugs and nods, grateful that she understands.*

GAIL: Go back in. Have fun with your mates. Give your poor old brain a rest.

GAIL *kisses* ZAC *on the temple tenderly. He lets her.*

JYSSYNTAH *and* MARISSA *come outside, giggly and overexcited, calling to* MATT *to follow them.* ZAC *escapes them by hurrying inside after* GAIL.

JYSSYNTAH *turns her back on* MARISSA *in order to flirt madly with* MATT. MARISSA *is stranded, bored. When* RILEY *comes outside, mucking around on his board, she watches him.*

MARISSA: That looks fun.

RILEY: Have a go on my board if you like. Get the feel of it.

MARISSA *puts one foot on the board, sliding it back and forth.*

RILEY: Put your feet sideways like—yeah, that's right.

MARISSA *giggles, enjoying it.* JYSSYNTAH *is still busy flirting with* MATT.

JYSSYNTAH: We should go back to your place after this.

MATT:	I dunno…
JYSSYNTAH:	Get some beers and UDL cans on the way.
MATT:	How are you gonna get—?
JYSSYNTAH:	Buy them at the drive-in bottle shop. I can pass for eighteen. Easily.
MATT:	But everyone in Narra knows you. Knows you're fifteen.
JYSSYNTAH:	Yeah, but couldn't we—?

MATT *laughs and ducks out of the way as* MARISSA *lurches past on the skateboard.*

JYSSYNTAH:	Hello! Have you gone mental?
MARISSA:	I was just having a—
JYSSYNTAH:	So embarrassing. I can't believe I'm being seen with you. Oh, my God.

MARISSA *jumps off the board.*

MARISSA:	I wasn't really—I just—

MARISSA *scuttles obediently over to join* JYSSYNTAH.

JYSSYNTAH:	[*to* MATT, *rolling her eyes about* MARISSA] Sorry.
MATT:	Look, anyway, I might head home. Got work in the morning.

MATT *wanders off.*

JYSSYNTAH:	[*bitterly disappointed*] Thanks a lot, Marissa. Thanks for stuffing things up with me and Matt.
MARISSA:	What? I never did anything.
JYSSYNTAH:	First you do that stupid act which, y'know, makes me look stupid—as your friend. And then you stood there like a brain-dead goldfish.

JYSSYNTAH *stalks off.* MARISSA *scurries after her.*

MARISSA:	Jyssyntah, wait…

COREY *crosses the courtyard, looking for* LAUREN. *He finds her as she wanders outside.*

    COREY: There you are.

    LAUREN: Hi.

    COREY: Can I get you something? More pizza? A drink?

    LAUREN: No thanks, I've had heaps.

They lean against a wall in awkward silence.

    COREY: You know, there's one bad thing about us getting the skatepark.

    LAUREN: What could be bad? We turned the town around. We won.

    COREY: Yeah. It's mad. Brilliant. But now the campaign's finished, I won't get to see you.

    LAUREN: We go to the same school, deadhead. Anyway, you can't avoid seeing people in a town as small as Narra.

    COREY: Won't be the same as when we were working on that stuff. That was good.

    LAUREN: It was good.

COREY *lets a silence go by.*

    COREY: I really like you.

    LAUREN: Well, I really like you.

COREY *takes a deep breath for courage and leans in for a kiss.* LAUREN *ducks her head away to avoid being kissed.*

    LAUREN: Sorry. I just—

    COREY: Oh no, I'm sorry—I didn't mean to—

    LAUREN: I just don't know if I'm—I mean, I really want us to be friends.

    COREY: Yeah, yeah. We're friends. Sorry if I—

They overlap embarrassed apologies until the noisy pack of kids barging outside interrupts.

JT: Photo! Photo! Come on! Everyone!

The whole lot spill outside into the courtyard, being herded into a group by JT, *armed with a camera.*

JT: Come on! Historic occasion. Gotta have a photo! Bunch up!

Too embarrassed to meet each other's eye, LAUREN *and* COREY *are caught up in the photo group. Ad libs from* JT *and others as they try to fit everyone in, get the heights right, etc.* LAUREN *gets squashed up close to* ZAC. *They both freeze, hating it, but they are stuck.*

JT: Oh—hang on, sorry folks. Forgot to turn the flash bizzo on.

Roars of abuse at JT.

JT: Won't take long.

The group breaks up again. COREY *and* ZAC *end up in a corner on their own for a moment.*

ZAC: Any luck with—uh—?

He indicates LAUREN.

COREY: Nuh. Someone must've told her I'm a repulsive dog. She goes: 'Let's be friends.'

ZAC: Oh, mate…

COREY: Oh, well, there's always hope. 'Just friends' is a start. The impossible can happen.

GAIL: [*to* COREY] You coming to stay at our place after?

COREY: No thanks. Might head home. Cheer Mum up with the good news.

GAIL: She'll be pleased, yeah.

COREY: Surprised, more like. She said it'd never happen. We couldn't do it. But we did, eh. [*He takes a deep breath, high on the triumph of the day.*] Ha! I can't believe how good this feels. Like, we did it and it worked.

ZAC *nods, pleased to see* COREY *so happy.* COREY *closes his eyes, arms extended, and sucks in a deep breath.*

_____COREY: I don't wanna ever forget feeling this good, you know?

_____JT: Okay! Ready! Quick! Before I stuff up the camera again. Bunch up. Ugly people in the dark areas. Smile!

Grins as the flash goes off.

The group disperses, with the skating pack making the restaurant disappear and taking us into the schoolyard:

SCENE EIGHT

Schoolyard. Daytime.

The skaters grab schoolbags, yank on school ties and take up their positions in the yard. The mood is sombre.

_____STELLA: Narra High.

_____TRAVIS: What a hole.

MATT *walks across the yard, head down, grim.*

_____MITCHELL: I was the first person who saw the cops turn up.

_____JT: No way. I was in Design and Tech. I saw them first, through the windows—

_____TRAVIS: [*snapping, aggressive*] Doesn't matter who saw the cops first.

TRAVIS'*s sharp tone makes them all suddenly quiet and grim.*

_____MITCHELL: It didn't take long for the rumours to start going round.

STELLA: Rumours about what happened.

STELLA *and* AMY *are too upset to tell the story.*

JYSSYNTAH: First off, just about how there'd been a shooting and that.

TRAVIS: But no one knew who—like, who got shot and who did it.

JT: Apparently, they found Warren Beggs' body—

RILEY: Corey's stepdad.

JYSSYNTAH: He was lying in the front yard.

MITCHELL: So to begin with they thought it might be a drive- by shooting or whatever.

JT: On account of Warren Beggs being involved in drugs and stuff.

JYSSYNTAH: But then inside the house, they found Corey's mum. She'd been shot.

TRAVIS: And then the cops went in the kitchen.

JT: Found Corey.

TRAVIS *is now too upset to speak.*

MITCHELL: They reckon Warren Beggs shot Corey first—

JT: Some people reckon Corey was stopping Warren from hitting his mum.

JYSSYNTAH: But no one knows for sure.

MITCHELL: Next he shot Corey's mum.

JT: Then he shot himself.

RILEY: To begin with, we're all going: 'No way. That's not true.'

MITCHELL: 'That's just a dumb story. Someone taking the piss.'

RILEY: Then Zac got called up to the principal's office.

STELLA: Because the teachers knew he was Corey's best friend.

ZAC *walks across the yard to the principal's office. The other kids fall silent, watching* ZAC, *the reality sinking in for them.*

MITCHELL: That's when we knew the story was true.

RILEY: And Corey was really dead.

MITCHELL: Murdered.

JYSSYNTAH: Everyone came out of classes. I mean, how could you go on blahing about Geography or Maths or whatever?

MITCHELL: All round the school, people were crying.

STELLA *puts an arm around* AMY's *shoulders as they walk across the yard, both of them crying.*

RILEY: I still couldn't believe it. Even after the principal announced it at assembly.

JYSSYNTAH: Corey was just a kid. He couldn't be dead. No way.

LAUREN *walks across the yard, upset.*

RILEY: Was she his girlfriend?

MITCHELL: They hung round together a lot. She might've been his girlfriend.

JYSSYNTAH: I saw them together on the night when—

JYSSYNTAH *stops and stares as* GAIL *walks on.*

MITCHELL: The school called parents to pick up the kids who were the most torn up.

GAIL *sits and talks for a moment with* CONSTABLE ALEXAKIS.

GAIL: They rang me at work. I thought something terrible had happened to Zac. My heart was pounding that hard, I probably wasn't safe to drive. When I heard about Corey, my first reaction was relief—that my own son was okay.

ALEXAKIS: That's natural, Gail. You shouldn't—

GAIL: I feel bad about feeling that. But that's the truth of it. [*Looking around the school*] I went to Narra High with his mum. Trisha.

ALEXAKIS: I didn't know that.

GAIL: Yeah. She left part way through Year Ten. Got into trouble with the cops in Sydney, we heard. Then in Year Twelve, I got pregnant. With Zac. Turned out Trisha got pregnant that same year.

ALEXAKIS: It looks like Corey was defending his mum when it happened.

GAIL *nods.*

GAIL: Bloody Trisha. I hate her guts right now. If she was here right now, I'd shake her, I'd shout, I'd—Why couldn't she be a better mother to that boy?

ZAC *walks back across the yard.* GAIL *jumps up to go to him.* ZAC *puts his hands up—he doesn't want that—and walks off.*

JT: Next day, this whole platoon of counsellors swarmed over the school.

TRAVIS: Even people who weren't really Corey's friends were bawling in class and seeing the counsellors.

JYSSYNTAH: Some of them were just trying to get attention.

MITCHELL: But lots of kids were upset for real.

RILEY: Just to think that could happen to a kid. A kid we all knew.

JT: Something like that—it blows the universe apart.

TRAVIS: The bad guy won.

MITCHELL: And it was like nothing good would ever happen in this town again.

The skaters pull on bits of black clothing as they move us into the next scene.

STELLA: The counsellors stayed around for the rest of that week.

MITCHELL: Until Corey's funeral.

TRAVIS: Which was a total bloody joke.

SCENE NINE

A street outside the church as people file out after the funeral. All the kids are there, as well as ZAC, LAUREN, GAIL *and* MATT.

STELLA: It felt like the funeral had nothing to do with Corey or any of us.

MITCHELL: None of Corey's friends did speeches or anything.

TRAVIS: Just some minister blabbing on about God.

JT: [*as the minister*] Oh, Lord, we beseech thee, blah blah.

JYSSYNTAH: I couldn't understand what the minister guy was saying half the time.

RILEY: Hardly even mentioned Corey.

TRAVIS: You'd look at Corey's coffin and think… I dunno… you'd think—

MITCHELL: Then we'd have to sing some hymn and you wouldn't have a chance to think.

JT: A lot of the 'respectable' people in Narra never even went.

MATT: Didn't want to be associated with the Matthews and what happened.

JYSSYNTAH: Mind you, the stickybeaks showed up.

MITCHELL: Oh yeah, going to funerals is a hobby for some people in Narragindi.

STELLA: The gossip got going bigtime in the week after Corey was killed.

The skaters mimic various townspeople—smug, outraged, snide, curious:

'Apparently she was going to leave Beggs. That's what started it.'

'The boy—Corey—he was definitely involved in the drug dealing.'

'I heard Trisha Matthews found out about Warren getting the boy into drugs and that's what the argument was about.'

'No, no, no, she was in it up to her neck. It was her idea.'

'Violent temper, Corey Matthews. You wouldn't know it to look at him. That's probably what got his mother killed.'

'Yeah, if it wasn't this it would've been something else. He was always going to end up in strife, that kid.'

'Good riddance to bad rubbish. A few less druggos in the world.'

LAUREN *comes out of the funeral. She runs into* RAY STONE. *He holds out his hands to her.*

RAY: Lauren.

She lets him take her hands. A bit of sympathy makes her crumple into tears again.

RAY: This must be very upsetting for you. I'm sorry.

LAUREN: Thanks, Uncle Ray.

RAY: You shouldn't have to deal with something as sordid as this.

LAUREN: [*teary, confused*] Sorry?

RAY: You've got a soft heart, Lauren. But that's not always a good thing. I tried to warn you about getting involved.

LAUREN: [*pulling back from him*] What? Corey was my—

RAY: Yes, it's a sad business. But the truth of it is that boy was always likely to end up—

LAUREN: Stop. Please don't say any more.

RAY: Lauren—

LAUREN: I said shut up. I don't want to hear one more word out of your mouth.

LAUREN's *fierce stare makes* RAY *back off and go.*

When LAUREN *turns around, she sees* ZAC *leaving the church. They exchange a look—full of pain but no use to each other.* LAUREN *goes.*

GAIL *hurries to catch up with* ZAC *as he walks away.*

GAIL: Zac. Don't do this. Don't walk out on school. Don't—

ZAC: I told you. I was only hanging round for the funeral and then I'm gone.

GAIL: I know you feel like—

ZAC: Have you seen the vultures in this town all round the carcass?

GAIL: I know.

ZAC: It's bad enough people in Narra never did anything to help Corey when he was alive, but now he's dead they pour mud all over him and tear down who he really was.

GAIL: Zac, there are good and bad people everywhere. If you leave, there'll be bad people anywhere you go—

ZAC: But at least I won't have to look at their faces every day and know who they are and know what they think when I walk down the street.

ZAC *can't let himself look at her as he walks away.*

The skaters take us away from the funeral.

STELLA: We ended up back at the steps that day.

JT: Nowhere else to go…

SCENE TEN

Town Hall steps/streets.

The group assembles limply around the steps but there's no energy, no interest in skating.

    TRAVIS: But without Corey—

    RILEY: And without Zac—

    JT: Didn't seem much point.

The sound of the horn from Travis's brother's car.

    TRAVIS: I'm off.

The others call 'see ya' as TRAVIS *goes with his brother.*

    STELLA: Everything pretty much fell apart after that.

    JT: We heard Zac went to live with his cousin in Glen.

    JYSSYNTAH: The story was, he was going to hang out there for a while and then head to Sydney to look for work.

    JT: Zac's mum always used to be a really nice lady—

    RILEY: Always joking with kids and that.

    JT: Now, when you went into ChemistZone, she was really tooshy.

    AARON: Didn't smile.

    JT: Didn't hardly look at you.

LAUREN *walks past, making a vague hello to* AMY, RILEY *and* STELLA.

    MITCHELL: Lauren was different after Corey died.

    JYSSYNTAH: Yeah, even Princess Lauren was going off the rails at school.

    MARISSA: Wagging classes.

    STELLA: Getting pissed off with teachers.

    MITCHELL: Suddenly sobbing her guts out in the corridor—

    JYSSYNTAH: And then locking herself in the girls' toilets.

    JT: Travis started hanging round with his brother and his mates.

    STELLA: Pack of brain-dead idiots.

    JT: Travis was with those guys when they held up

the service station on the highway to Glen.

STELLA: With a shotgun.

JYSSYNTAH: Those morons held up the servo in a town where everyone knows them.

STELLA: Brain-dead.

MITCHELL: Got caught, of course.

MATT: Travis spent a night in the cells.

JT: He reckons it wasn't so bad.

JYSSYNTAH: Oh, sure. Luxury, I bet. He'd've been shit-scared.

JT: Yeah. I reckon.

MITCHELL: Travis is in bigtime trouble now. Went to court in Glen.

JT: He's home now.

MITCHELL: But once he's had the trial, he'll probably have to go to kiddie jail.

STELLA: He stopped coming to school.

JYSSYNTAH: We don't see him round anymore.

JT: Just when it looked like things couldn't get any more shithouse—

MATT: The council did what Zac always said they'd do.

STELLA: Doublecrossed us on the skatepark.

RILEY: Even though we had the OzYouth money and everything.

MATT: The council said we couldn't put it in the park.

JT *brandishes a local newspaper with a banner headline.*

JT: 'No Genuine Youth Interest in Skatepark, Says Council.'

STELLA: Which is total crap.

MITCHELL: But they can tell whatever lies they want.

The group disperses, muttering about 'nothing you can do', 'what's the point?'.

RILEY: You know the awesome skateboard Mitchell won in the raffle?

JT: He never even took the plastic off.

STELLA: Mitchell reckons he's going to sell it back to the shop.

The few who remain create Glenthorpe Park during the following:

RILEY: Lauren was the only person who even talked about fighting for the skatepark.

STELLA: Some people said that was because she wanted to get back at her uncle.

JYSSYNTAH: A lot of arguments round Lauren's house, apparently.

MARISSA: People in their street heard the yelling.

JT: Some people reckon it was because she was still so cut up about Corey.

STELLA: Who knows. The point is, the next weekend, Lauren caught the bus down to Glen…

SCENE ELEVEN

Glenthorpe Park.
ZAC *is there alone, mucking around on his board.* LAUREN *appears, watching him until he spots her and stops.*

ZAC: Hi.

LAUREN: Hi.

ZAC: You doing more filming for your video?

LAUREN: No. Your cousin told me I'd find you down here.

ZAC: Oh right…

LAUREN: You heard they pulled the plug on the skatepark.

ZAC: Yeah.

LAUREN: So everyone's given up.

ZAC: Worn out. Exactly what those old bastards want.

LAUREN *reaches into a bag to bring out the skatepark model* ZAC *had given* COREY.

LAUREN: The police didn't know what to do with this. I said I'd give it back to you.

ZAC *takes the model.*

LAUREN: Look, I know you hate my guts.

ZAC: I don't hate your guts.

LAUREN: What happened to Corey... I still can't even... I don't know who I can talk to or what I—

ZAC: Corey's dead. Nothing to talk about.

LAUREN: I guess not, but I just wanted—

ZAC: I was thinking... if the skatepark ever got built in Narra—never prob'ly—but if it had, it should've been dedicated to Corey.

LAUREN: You mean, like 'The Corey Matthews Memorial Skatepark'?

ZAC: Something like that, yeah.

LAUREN: That'd be fantastic.

ZAC: No point now. If the skatepark's stuffed.

LAUREN: Well, maybe it's not stuffed if we can prove to everyone that—

ZAC: Why are you saying 'we'? Don't look at me.

LAUREN: I'm not a skater. I'm not the person who can get everyone psyched about the skatepark again.

ZAC: I said don't look at me.

LAUREN: But if we could get the Corey Matthews Memorial Skatepark, it'd be—I mean, you know how important the skatepark was to Corey—

ZAC: [*snapping at her*] Skatepark's not gonna do Corey any good now.

LAUREN *falls silent.* ZAC *puts the model down on the ground.*

ZAC: I don't want that thing.

_____LAUREN: Corey loved it. He always—
_____ZAC: I said I don't want it.

LAUREN *kicks the model across the ground toward him.*

_____LAUREN: Fuck you then. Stomp on it, chuck it in the river. Do whatever you want with it. I don't care.

LAUREN *goes.*

As the kids remove Glenthorpe Park, ZAC *walks off, picking the model up as he goes.*

_____MITCHELL: The council called a public meeting.
_____RILEY: On the spot where the skatepark was supposed to go.
_____JYSSYNTAH: Everyone was going:
_____JT: 'Why? Skatepark's dead in the water.'
_____STELLA: 'It's over.'
_____JT: 'What's the meeting in aid of?'
_____MITCHELL: So the council could spin some PR bullshit to explain why they pulled the plug on—
_____JYSSYNTAH: To explain to all the people who donated money and bought raffle tickets and that—
_____MITCHELL: To prove that kids didn't care much about a skatepark.
_____JT: Yeah, well, they can stuff their public meeting right up their—
_____STELLA: Yeah, we all know it'd be some trick.
_____JT: So no point showing up and let them make fools out of us.

SCENE TWELVE

The skatepark site.
RAY STONE *walks on, checks his watch, brisk.* GAIL, AMY *and* RILEY

are there, anxiously looking around.

AMY: Isn't anyone else gonna show up?

RILEY: Aaron said he might come.

GAIL: I was hoping Stella would be here.

AMY: Umm… I saw her at netball and she said, 'We'll never get a skatepark.'

GAIL: Yeah, well, that's what all the kids think. Can't blame them. Why should they turn up here and get disappointed? Again.

RILEY: There's someone.

GAIL *turns, hopeful, to see a bloke approaching—*DENNIS.

GAIL: Oh—no, that's Dennis from the newspaper. Must be doing a story about this meeting.

DENNIS *walks up, with notebook and camera.*

DENNIS: G'day, Ray. Gail. Kids.

RAY: Ah, Dennis. Don't think you'll get much of a story out of this for the *Narra News*.

RAY *shakes his hand firmly and they have a quiet chat.*

RAY: [*to* GAIL] Is this all you expect in the way of a turn-out?

GAIL *shrugs, hopeless.* RAY *speechifies for the benefit of* DENNIS, *who takes notes.*

RAY: Look, Dennis mate, the reason I offered this public meeting is to make it abundantly clear that council's decision to reject the skatepark is not based on anti-youth feeling—

LAUREN, *unseen until now, heckles loudly.*

LAUREN: Yeah it is. You know it is.

RAY *is annoyed but pointedly ignores her.*

RAY: Fact of the matter is, there's no genuine youth interest in a skatepark—

LAUREN: Lie. Big fat lie.

RAY: Narragindi does not want an eyesore in the middle of town, unused except as a centre for anti-social behaviour. See for yourself, Dennis—the poor turn-out today is powerful evidence that the town youth don't want this skatepark—

GAIL, *who's been controlling herself, blurts out at him.*

GAIL: Because you bastards wore the kids down. Made them lose any faith that things could be fair. I always said to my kids—if you want something, you can work to make it happen. What am I supposed to say to them now?

RAY: Look, I think—uh—

GAIL: Why? That's what's got me buggered. Some of you lot just love the sound of the word 'no'. Then there are the fence-sitters—want to keep everybody happy. Fence-jumper types end up losing their balls on the barbed wire.

RAY: Gail, the truth is—

GAIL *is too fiery and upset to be talked down.*

GAIL: Then I worked it out. You lot straight-out hate kids. The way you go on, you'd think every kid was a thug and a criminal.

RAY: What I want to see for this town—

GAIL: What you want is put all the kids—well, the boys—put all the boys in an underground bunker when they hit twelve and not let them out till they turn eighteen, ready to be workers and members of the RSL. Skaters and their mates—they're our kids. This town's children. We owe them a bit more than this bullshit.

RAY: [*to* DENNIS] You can see here how recent events

have unsettled our community. Frankly, I think there's a lot of grief and anger being transferred where it doesn't belong. It's not our fault that boy got himself killed.

GAIL: Got himself—? What did you say?

GAIL *is upset, speechless.* AMY *puts an arm around her.*

AMY: Let's just go home, Mum.

GAIL, AMY *and* RILEY *start to walk away, defeated.* RAY *goes over to* DENNIS, *smug.*

RAY: Mate, truth is it was an orchestrated campaign— the work of a small, noisy group and even then, largely pushed by one adult with her own agenda. If you want to have a squizz at the report we—

DENNIS: What's that noise?

In the sudden silence, we can hear the scraping sound of wheels on concrete.

AMY *and* RILEY *laugh—they know what the sound is. The sound gets closer, then we see skaters and BMXers descend on the site from various directions. (Our skating pack includes* TRAVIS, *plus as many others as we can have. The non-skaters, like* JYSSYNTAH, MITCHELL *and* MARISSA, *could be on foot or getting doubled.)*

They all call out 'G'day, Mr Stone' as they arrive.

ZAC *zooms through to the front of the pack.*

ZAC: There's more on their way from the footy ground. Another forty or fifty, I reckon. Why'd you set the meeting the same time as the football semi-final, Mr Stone?

RAY: Look, I'm not interested in grandstanding or silly stunts or—

JT *hands* ZAC *a stack of papers.*

ZAC: [*to* DENNIS] Hi. Dunno if you'd be interested in

these. Letters of support for the skatepark. So far, we got about—

_____ JT: About sixty.

_____ ZAC: Plus there's a petition. Two hundred signatures so far, but we haven't had much time.

DENNIS *takes the papers and looks over them.*

_____ JT: [*to* DENNIS] Cool camera. Hey, what about a photo of the Narra youth who aren't interested in a skatepark?

_____ DENNIS: Why not?

The skaters dive in to form a tableau so DENNIS *can take a photo.* ZAC *signals to* GAIL *and* LAUREN *to join the group.*

RAY *walks off, making a mobile call, as* DENNIS *takes photos.*

From left: Jessica Tuckwell as Jyssyntah, Alex Vaughan (obscured) as Marissa, Richard Kessell as Zac, Robert Scurry as Dennis, Anthony Gooley as Ray and Jonathan Latham as Riley in the 2003 atyp production. (Photo: Phil Sheather)

Between cheesy grins, the skaters take up the story.

JT: Made the front page of the *Narra News*.

MITCHELL: The paper ran a big campaign in support of the skatepark.

TRAVIS: Next thing we knew—

STELLA: Council changed their mind about the skatepark.

JT: It's a miracle!

MITCHELL: Few people must've jumped the fence.

JT: [*wincing, cradling his balls*] Crikey, watch out for the barbed wire as you go over.

RILEY: They poured the concrete slab for the skatepark two weeks later.

A burst of energetic activity as the skaters assemble the Narragindi skatepark.

They all rush about during the following dialogue—building, landscaping, etc. (including LAUREN *and* ZAC*).*

MITCHELL: We went for the pre-cast concrete ramps. Two quarter pipes, couple of vert ramps, a pretty decent funbox.

STELLA: [*rolling her eyes*] The Expert.

TRAVIS: Exactly like the plans Zac drew when he was twelve. Which is kinda cool, eh.

JT: Lauren and Zac—they organised the sign to dedicate the skatepark to Corey.

LAUREN: [*to* ZAC] Best thing is if we unveil the sign at the official opening. When everyone's there.

ZAC: For sure. So we have to work out the exact wording we want on the sign.

TRAVIS: [*to the audience*] A few of us went: 'Oh, wouldn't it be sick to organise a skating competition as part of the opening day.'

STELLA: So we did.

_____ JT:	[*grandly*] The Corey Matthews Skatepark Grand Opening Skate Competition.
_____ MITCHELL:	Lauren got on the phone to the big skate gear companies—
_____ JT:	To see if she could scrounge some decent prizes out of them.
_____ STELLA:	She raved on about how the opening day competition was a 'great publicity opportunity'.
_____ RILEY:	She goes:

LAUREN *pretends to talk into a phone, sending up her pushy tone:*

_____ LAUREN:	'The Narra skatepark is a classic good news story.'
_____ MITCHELL:	She really put the pressure on those guys.
_____ LAUREN:	'This is your chance to give something back by sponsoring grassroots skating, not just flashy pros.'
_____ ZAC:	[*grinning*] So bossy.
_____ LAUREN:	You having a go at me again?
_____ ZAC:	Bossy in a good way.

LAUREN *blushes. He's looking at her. She's saved by* AMY.

_____ AMY:	We better hurry up, you guys. [*Explaining to the audience*] The opening celebration is, like, tomorrow.

AMY *and other kids are decorating the skatepark for the opening and doing final touches to the landscaping.*

The last bits of the skatepark are swung into place with a flourish.

_____ JT:	Da da!
_____ STELLA:	Finished.

RILEY *is hopping around with ants in his pants.*

_____ RILEY:	I can't wait till tomorrow. I won't be able to sleep tonight. I know I won't.

LAUREN: Everyone got their list of jobs to do for tomorrow?

General noises of agreement to this.

LAUREN: Well, don't all stand around scratching your bums and looking at it. Get going on your jobs.

The pack zooms off—with ad libs teasing about LAUREN *being bossy and kids yelling 'goodbye', 'see you tomorrow'.*

LAUREN, ZAC *and* AMY *are left behind, finishing something.*

LAUREN *looks up to see* ZAC *frozen for a minute, staring at the skatepark.*

LAUREN: Did you ever think we'd get it?

ZAC *shakes his head and they exchange a smile. They break the look, embarrassed, and throw themselves back into the job they're doing.*

GAIL *arrives. Unseen, she watches* ZAC *for a moment, before approaching.*

AMY: Doesn't it look fantastic, Mum?

GAIL: Yep. Fantastic, Amy.

ZAC *can see his mum's grim mood.*

ZAC: What's up?

GAIL: Bad news.

ZAC: No one can pull the plug on the skatepark now. We're standing in it.

GAIL: I thought the sign—I thought dedicating the park to Corey was just a formality, but—

ZAC: But what?

GAIL: The council knocked it back.

LAUREN: I don't get it—

GAIL: They won't let us dedicate the park to Corey.

AMY: They can't do that!

GAIL: Well, they can.

LAUREN: Did they say why?

GAIL: Something about what's appropriate for—

ZAC: It doesn't matter why.

ZAC *throws down the tools he was holding, as if they're contaminated. The violent sound makes the others jump.*

GAIL: I'm not going to tell everyone yet. I don't want to spoil the big day.

ZAC *doesn't respond.*

GAIL: We've still got the opening tomorrow. We've still got—

ZAC: What's the point? Why would I want to be here tomorrow? I don't want to be part of any—

GAIL: I know you're upset—

ZAC: I don't want anything to do with this fucking skatepark.

ZAC *heads off.*

GAIL: Don't shut down and not talk to me. Don't do that to me again.

ZAC *stops but he won't look at her.*

GAIL: I thought—when it happened—when Corey died—I thought: okay, Gail, you better hold yourself together through all this—so when Zac's ready to talk, you can... oh, I don't know. I miss him. I miss him so much. And I feel guilty. Why didn't I make him stay over that weekend? Why didn't I ring the cops and say—? I don't know what... I should've scooped him up and mothered him and... I should've kept him safe. You were a good, good friend to Corey—

ZAC *shakes his head.*

GAIL: Yes you were. I was so proud of you for that. Now I don't know what to say to you. About why things happen. Something like that can happen to Corey and there's... And I don't know what I can say to my own kid.

GAIL *is so upset that* AMY *rushes forward to comfort her.*

AMY: [*to* ZAC] Don't make Mum cry again, you dirtbag. Why can't you just come to the opening tomorrow and—?

GAIL: Leave him, Amy. He doesn't have to be part of it if he doesn't want to.

ZAC *goes.* GAIL, AMY *and* LAUREN *go off in the opposite direction.*

A COUNCIL WORKER *comes on to install the park sign. It just reads* 'NARRAGINDI SHIRE COUNCIL SKATEPARK' *with lots of small-print prohibitions—no littering, no loud music, etc.*

Night falls on the skatepark.

Felicity Ward as Gail and Richard Kessell as Zac in the 2003 atyp production. (Photo: Phil Sheather)

SCENE THIRTEEN

Park. Night.

LAUREN *finds* ZAC *hunched up in the darkness under a tree and sits down near him. They sit in silence for a moment.*

ZAC:	Why did I think some stupid kids' skatepark would make anything feel right?
LAUREN:	Corey's still dead.
ZAC:	Yeah. People in this town loved it—the murders. Not everyone, I'm not saying everyone. But a lot of them felt better after what happened to Corey and his mum—seeing bad things happen to people they think are scum—
LAUREN:	It makes them feel safer.
ZAC:	Safer. That's it. Not that I can feel superior.
LAUREN:	What do you mean?

ZAC *shrugs, clamming up.*

LAUREN:	At least you didn't hurt his feelings. The night of the party, he kind of—well, he wanted to kiss me and he said—
ZAC:	I know.
LAUREN:	You do? Oh. I think I just got scared. And now I can't take that back or change my mind or—I mean, that was the last time I saw him.
ZAC:	But you didn't know that—
LAUREN:	No… Doesn't mean I don't feel guilty.

ZAC *looks at her. Maybe he can really talk to her.*

ZAC:	Before, I was pissed off with the world but there was no target, no reason—not enough of a reason anyway.
LAUREN:	Yeah, I do remember.
ZAC:	Then when Corey died, it was—oh, you're gonna

LAUREN: think I'm even more of a dick that you already do—

LAUREN: I don't think that.

ZAC: It was like I had a target now. I could be angry about what happened to Corey. And it was sort of a relief, you know?

LAUREN: I think I get you.

ZAC: How fucked is that? My best friend gets murdered and in a weird, screwed-up way, it makes me feel better...

LAUREN: But that's not the only thing you felt—

ZAC: No. Oh no. Also felt sorry for myself bigtime. Poor little Zac. He misses his friend Corey.

LAUREN: You're allowed to, aren't you?

ZAC: I make myself sick. What right have I got to feel sorry for myself about Corey when he—? I mean, I'm so lucky compared to him. Even before. He was a good person and he had fuck-all... The world gave him no chance. It's not fair me being so lucky, having so much, when Corey—it's not right—it's...

ZAC *is breathless as terrible sobs overtake him.* LAUREN *reaches across to comfort him. Both crying, they lean against each other for support.*

After a few moments, they find themselves face to face and begin to kiss. Both give in to the kiss until ZAC *jumps to his feet, screwing up his face in self-disgust.*

ZAC: Ohh, no. No. He wanted to be with you and— No, it's not right. I'm sorry, you know. It's not your problem or—Nothing's ever just right.

Why can't anything be right? Everything's fucked. So what's the point? The whole universe is fucked.

ZAC disappears into the darkness and LAUREN *eventually goes off in the other direction.*

SCENE FOURTEEN

One streetlight casts a feeble light over the deserted skatepark.

ZAC *approaches it. He kicks the new council sign but gets no satisfaction from that. He is about to wander away when he hears something. A scrape of wheels.*

He turns back to see COREY, *just visible in the dim light, standing on top of a ramp.* COREY *drops in and whooshes down and up the other ramp.* ZAC *watches him skate back and forth.* COREY *tries a few tricks but mostly just enjoys himself, laid-back and contented.*

At the end of one run, COREY *flips up and disappears down the far bank out of view.* ZAC *follows and jumps down the back of the ramp where* COREY *went.*

SCENE FIFTEEN

The skatepark. Daytime.

A flurry of activity and excitement as the pack of skaters sweep on, bringing streamers, balloons, tables of food, a music system, maybe a Lions Club sausage sizzle, maybe a few stalls selling commercial skategear, etc.

JT:	The big opening day. People started turning up for the skate competition.
STELLA:	Lauren scrounged truly excellent prizes so we got a good turn-out for the skating competition.
TRAVIS:	Skaters from Glen and other towns across the

state.

MATT: Plus a few guys from Victoria.

RILEY: There's that guy from Glen—what's his name?

TRAVIS: That guy? He's a wanker.

JT: Mate, he's a wanker who can do a 360 nollie flip.

RILEY: Zac could beat him easy.

JT: Yeah, Zac's our only chance for Narra to beat Glen in that event.

JYSSYNTAH: No bigname sponsored guys turned up or anything.

RILEY: Who cares? It was the most fantastic day in the history of Narra.

General agreement on that.

JT: Shame about the sign.

STELLA: Yeah, it was a bummer.

Blake Bowden as Corey in the 2003 atyp production. (Photo: Phil Sheather)

TRAVIS: Those maggots on the council wouldn't put Corey's name on their poxy sign.

They stare at the sign, cursing under their breath.

JYSSYNTAH *gasps at something she sees offstage.*

JYSSYNTAH: Oh—my—God.

MARISSA *rolls slowly onto the skatepark on a skateboard. She giggles, nervous but happy.* RILEY *trots alongside her, coaching and steadying her.*

RILEY: That's it. That's heaps good. Be ready to do an ollie soon.

JYSSYNTAH: Are you trying to look like a sad, sad retard? Is that your big plan?

MARISSA *rolls past* JYSSYNTAH, *ignoring her.*

JYSSYNTAH: Did you hear me, Marissa? I hope you know how tragic you look. I hope you know that I can't be seen with you in public if you're going to embarrass me to death in front of my friends. Marissa? Are you deaf? Marissa!

MARISSA *rolls past with* RILEY *guiding her.*

MARISSA: [*to* RILEY] Can you hear anything?

RILEY: Nuh. Can't hear anything.

MARISSA: Me neither.

MARISSA *grins and rolls out of sight to* JYSSYNTAH'*s disgust. Then* JT *spots something offstage and hoots with amazement.*

JT: Hello! What do we have here? Am I seeing things?

STELLA *beckons to someone offstage.*

STELLA: Come on. You have to come over and face everyone sometime.

JT: Ladies and gents, Narragindi's chances are

suddenly looking up!

MITCHELL *gingerly enters. He's dressed in skater clothes plus lots of protective gear—kneepads, elbowpads, helmet. He carries the board he won in the raffle.*

TRAVIS: So is this just a fashion show or are you atchally gonna skate?

STELLA: He's gonna skate.

MITCHELL: I dunno.

JT: Oh, Mitch, you've gotta skate. We've gotta see this. Best show all day.

STELLA: Hey. Watch it. JT. Travis. And anyone else. Don't bag Mitchell out.

TRAVIS: Since when did he skate?

STELLA: He's been practising out the back of my place.

JT: Secret lessons! You sneaky dog.

STELLA: He's worked hard and he deserves a fair go from you dickheads. Fair enough?

JT: Fair enough.

TRAVIS *splutters with suppressed laughter.*

STELLA: That means you too, Travis.

TRAVIS *is silenced by* STELLA's *stern look.*

STELLA: [*to* MITCHELL] Let's go over here and hope those losers grow a brain before we come back.

STELLA *takes* MITCHELL *off.*

JT *squats down to adjust something on his skateboard.* TRAVIS *looks at the scene around him, contented. For a moment it's just the two of them.* JT *is busy with his gear and doesn't pay full attention at first.*

TRAVIS: Y'know, it's really good—

JT: Getting the skatepark? For sure.

TRAVIS:	Yeah, but I was going to say—
JT:	Going to say it's really, really good.
TRAVIS:	Will ya let me finish?
JT:	Sorry, sorry.
TRAVIS:	It's good us guys hanging out doing whatever. Like nothing's changed.

JT *forgets the board and looks at* TRAVIS, *not used to* TRAVIS *being this emotional.*

JT: You scared about court and juvenile detention and that?

TRAVIS *nods. He's really scared.*

TRAVIS: But when I'm with you guys, I feel like I used to. Before. I can kid myself for a minute anyway.

JT *nods—he gets him. They stand there in companionable silence for a moment.*

JT: Wanna go over and give Mitchell a hard time?

TRAVIS: Yeah. Don't reckon we've bagged him out nearly enough yet.

TRAVIS *and* JT *head off together, bellowing to* MITCHELL.

AMY *and* GAIL *arrive.* GAIL *is trying to smile but she's clearly anxious and preoccupied.* AMY *is ready to skate but she's attentive to* GAIL, *holding her hand protectively.*

LAUREN *comes straight across to* GAIL.

LAUREN: Hi. Is Zac coming?

GAIL *shrugs, not hopeful.*

LAUREN: Anyway, congratulations for today. You made this happen.

GAIL: Well, thanks for your help, Lauren. Amy, we'd better get you registered for your event.

LAUREN: Oh, yeah, I'm supposed to be helping with the registrations.

GAIL, LAUREN *and* AMY *go to the registration table.* RAY STONE *strides around the skatepark, shaking hands with people. He encounters* CONSTABLE ALEXAKIS *in uniform and shakes her hand, heartily.*

RAY: G'day, Constable. Here to promote police/youth relations?

ALEXAKIS: Well, I wanted to see the skating and support the kids and—

RAY: Oh, yes, isn't this such a wonderful boost for the town youth? Bit of a bumpy road getting here, but now we've got all the factors in place—

ALEXAKIS: Oh. I thought you were—

RAY: There were some legitimate concerns in some quarters, but my basic support for the youth was rock solid. Few words in the right ears and now we have this wonderful facility. So—uh…

RAY'*s smarmy talk suddenly dries up when* ZAC *appears.*

ZAC'*s ready to skate. Head down, clearly wound up, he goes straight to* GAIL *and hugs her, apologetic.*

Next ZAC *finds* LAUREN.

ZAC: Sorry for being a dickhead last night.

LAUREN *shrugs—it's okay.*

LAUREN: I didn't know if you'd show up.

ZAC: Yeah, well, it's Corey's skatepark, whatever the sign says.

LAUREN: It is.

ZAC: Anyway, I've gotta beat that try-hard wanker from Glen.

ZAC *takes off his jacket and drapes it over the Narragindi Council sign, completely obscuring it. This is met with whoops of approval from the kids.* JT *rushes over to the music system.*

             JT: Louder! Music's gotta be mega-loud. We're hooligans, remember. Anti-social youth!

Music comes up really loud as the skatepark is filled with skating kids.

The music distorts and then fades as the opening day celebration is gradually dismantled and removed by the skating pack, as they take us into:

SCENE SIXTEEN

The skatepark. Summer day.

      STELLA: Zac ended up coming third in his event.

             JT: The wanker from Glen came second.

  MITCHELL: The winner was this little guy from Wiley Creek.

     TRAVIS: D'you see that tiny dude? He was a runt.

             JT: Awesome skater but.

       RILEY: How did he learn to skate like that in Wiley Creek?

      STELLA: Practises a helluva lot.

  MITCHELL: Plus natural talent.

     TRAVIS: Wiley Creek… they're all inbreds over there.

             JT: Pack of country bumpkins.

     TRAVIS: The judges were mental. The little runt kid wasn't even that good.

ZAC *enters and interrupts:*

        ZAC: Travis, don't talk crap. That kid was awesome. He'll be a pro skater by the time he's seventeen.

      STELLA: [*to the audience*] Zac stayed in town. He's staying on for Year Eleven after the summer holidays.

ZAC: [*calling offstage*] Did you get it?

LAUREN *enters carrying a cardboard box to join* ZAC *who's carrying a toolbox. The two of them work on something in a corner of the skatepark.*

MITCHELL: Me, Stella and Jyssyntah are doing Year Eleven too.

JT: When Travis went back to court, he got a good behaviour bond.

JYSSYNTAH: Which means he's gotta stay out of trouble or he goes to jail for real.

MITCHELL: He got a job cleaning up at the silos.

TRAVIS: Shit money and the boss is a maggot, so dunno how long I'll hack it.

STELLA: JT's going to start an apprenticeship with his uncle who's a carpenter.

TRAVIS: Jeez, mate, will they let you near electric saws and that?

JT: 'Course. They don't expect me to chew through the timber with my teeth.

TRAVIS: Whoa, JT and sharp tools. Remind me never to visit you at work when I'm not feeling lucky.

JT: You are a dead man, Travis.

JT *makes a show of going after* TRAVIS, *does a spectacular trip and lands sprawled out, cackling.*

STELLA: On stinking hot days, a lot of kids have a swim at the river.

MITCHELL: But apart from that we hang out here.

TRAVIS: Narra's still a hole.

RILEY: No, it's not.

JT: But now it's a hole with a skatepark.

RILEY: Which is excellent.

There's a drilling sound.

JT:	Zac! What are you doing?
ZAC:	Drilling this in.
LAUREN:	It's a plaque we got made. For Corey.

LAUREN *and* ZAC *install a metal plaque in the side wall of one of the ramps.*

JT:	What—the council said you've got permission to put up a plaque—?
ZAC:	No.
LAUREN:	We didn't ask the council.
ZAC:	We just decided to do it.

ZAC *takes a step back to let them see it.*

STELLA:	In memory of our mate Corey Matthews.
JT:	1987—2002.
TRAVIS:	That's excellent.
ZAC:	Yeah.

ZAC *keeps drilling as the skatepark fills with skating kids.*

THE END

www.currency.com.au

Visit Currency Press' website now to:

- Buy your books online
- Browse through our full list of titles, from plays to screenplays, books on theatre, film and music, and more
- Choose a play for your school or amateur performance group by cast size and gender
- Obtain information about performance rights
- Find out about theatre productions and other performing arts news across Australia
- For students, read our study guides
- For teachers, access syllabus and other relevant information
- Sign up for our email newsletter

The performing arts publisher

www.ingramcontent.com/pod-product-compliance
Lightning Source LLC
Chambersburg PA
CBHW041932090426
42744CB00017B/2024